THE COSTS OF THE CAR:

A Preliminary Study of the Environmental and Social Costs

Associated with Private Car Use in Ontario

Pollution Probe
12 Madison Ave.
Toronto, Ontario
M5R 2S1

October 1991

TABLE OF CONTENTS

Table of Contents (continued)

EXECUTIVE SUMMARY

Every year, approximately 48 million new cars come off the world's assembly lines. This is more than one car every second. Despite the hard economic times, it is expected that approximately 875,000 of these cars will be sold in Canada, or about one car for every 30 Canadians. North American society is heavily dependent on the car. This is reflected in the increasing numbers of highways, parking lots and suburbs. Ontario's economy is also dependent on the car:

The Ontario government's car-related revenue, from registration fees, gas taxes, etc. equals about $3,484 million each year.

The car and its supporting activities account for 9% of Canada's GDP, and 95% of the auto industry is located in Ontario.

47% of car-related jobs in Canada are in Ontario.

The price for Ontario's dependence on cars is, however, very high. Massive costs stem from the car's harmful impacts on land-use planning, the environment and human health. Pollution Probe's inventory of the car's many impacts shows that drivers pay only part of the costs that arise from the use of their cars; essentially, drivers are being subsidized to pollute Ontario's land, air and water.

The costs of the car are reflected in government spending:

Government car-related expenditures in Ontario are over $4.5 billion each year. This includes:

About $1,173 million each year in car-related interest on the provincial debt.

Federal, provincial and municipal governments spending of $1.9 billion on highway construction and maintenance in Ontario each year.

Federal government spending of roughly $5 million on road safety in Ontario each year.

Municipal spending in Ontario of about $500 million on car-related policing each year.

Ontario Provincial Police spending of about $226 million on car-related policing each year.

OHIP payments of about $80 million for car accident-related health care.

An estimated $646 million in health care costs in Ontario for disease attributable to car-related air pollution.

Over $20 million in direct subsidies to the auto and petroleum industries.

The costs of the car are also reflected in the large amount of environmental damage and waste due to the car:

Motor vehicles are responsible for 16% of man's contribution to global warming.

Car emissions are responsible for 20% of ground level ozone.

Car emissions are responsible for 13% of acid rain.

Roughly 500,000 vehicles are disposed of and 7-8 million scrap tires generated each year in Ontario.

The car is responsible for numerous human health costs:

Each year in Ontario, about 1,200 people are killed and 118,000 are injured in car accidents.

Lost productivity due to car accident injuries and deaths costs the Ontario economy $620 million and $112 million, respectively, each year.

As well, the car uses a large amount of Canada's resources:

The car uses approximately 31% of the petroleum industry's total refined output.

Canadians in major Canadian cities consume one and a half times more gasoline per capita than people in major European cities, and five times more than in major "westernized" Asian cities.

In total, the cost of the car is very high:

The estimated cost of the car to Ontario is over $8 billion per year. (Does not include costs of global warming, stress due to traffic congestion, car-related court costs, Ontario Ministry of the Environment car-related spending or individual ownership costs).

CUMULATIVE INVENTORY OF COSTS

Direct Costs:

1. Highway and road expenditures
2. Interest on provincial debt due to previous highway spending
3. Government spending on the environment (e.g. pollution control and clean-up)
4. Road safety
5. Health care
6. Policing
7. Court costs
8. Subsidies to companies

Individual Costs:

1. Ownership and operating costs, including maintenance, oil, tires, gasoline, insurance, registration, etc.

Hidden Costs:

1. Destruction of farmland, urban green space and habitats
2. Excessive energy costs from making and using the car, especially in areas of urban sprawl
3. Damage to air and water from mining
4. Air and soil pollution and contamination from smelting
5. Air and water pollution from drilling and processing petroleum
6. Water pollution from the production of petroleum-based chemicals
7. Damage from the transport of petroleum on land and water
8. Acidification of land and water from car emissions and auto industry smokestacks
9. Damage to plant and crop growth from elevated levels of ozone
10. The growing environmental and health costs of global warming
11. Damage to water and vegetation from the use of salt
12. Damage to air, land and water from the disposal of cars and their component parts
13. Damage to human health from regular discharge of toxins into lakes and rivers by the auto industry
14. Respiratory damage from elevated levels of SOx
15. Respiratory damage from elevated levels of ozone
16. Impaired coordination and heart damage from CO
17. Neurological damage from elevated levels of lead
18. Damage to skin and eyes from ozone depletion
19. Loss of time due to overcrowded highways
20. Stress and decline of quality of life
21. Unique costs to transportation disadvantaged
22. Financial costs due to lost productivity
23. Emotional damage to victims and families
24. Lack of R & D and spending for rural and public transit and alternative fuels

SUMMARY OF RECOMMENDATIONS

Recommendation 1
The province's Planning Act should be amended. Future planning should be based on five principles: (i) to intensify and concentrate development in areas that are already built up; (ii) to adopt minimum residential densities in developing areas; (iii) to limit office development to sites well served by public transit; (iv) to protect important farmland and natural areas; (v) to require that any new development, especially outside the Greater Toronto Area, include conditions for public transportation.

Recommendation 2
The proposed community of Seaton should not be built. It would be built on valuable farmland and many of its residents would work and shop in Toronto, making it another "bedroom" community.

Recommendation 3
In order to encourage land-use intensification, the province and City of Toronto should ensure that the Railway Lands are developed for residential units. Together with other new central area neighbourhoods and the "Main Streets" initiative, these residential areas will result in great energy savings and emission reductions.

Recommendation 4
Individuals should consider the environmental consequences of where and in what type of housing they choose to live. A conscious decision to live in areas which are already built up or to live in higher density housing is the best way to prevent urban sprawl.

Recommendation 5
The fuel economy of new cars should be upgraded. The federal and provincial governments should require automakers to meet a standard of 6.1 litres/100 km by the year 2000, and a standard of 5.0 litres/100 km by 2005. An increase in gasoline taxes may be needed to offset the incentive for increased driving as fuel efficient cars will go further on the same tank of gas. The revenue from the increased taxes should be used to fund a provincial vehicle inspection and maintenance program.

Recommendation 6
The fuel efficiency of cars already on Ontario's roads should be improved. An inspection and maintenance program should be set up by the provincial government with testing accompanying annual license renewal. Standards could vary with the age and type of car. Given the cost of such an operation, inspection could be on a random basis with the goal of testing 15-20% of all cars annually, or drivers could pay an inspection fee, as is the case for the Vancouver emission testing program. A fine for inefficient cars would provide an incentive for drivers to keep their cars tuned.

Recommendation 7
The recently imposed Tax for Fuel Conservation should be evaluated annually. The Ontario government should eliminate the flat tax rate ($75-$250) for cars with 6.0-9.4 litres/100 km fuel

efficiencies and instead set higher tax rates more closely tied to fuel efficiency for these cars.

Recommendation 8
Individuals should consider the environmental consequences of poor fuel efficiency when buying a car. A trendy sport utility vehicle, sports car or luxurious limousine with poor fuel economy is not a necessity in downtown Toronto.

Recommendation 9
The federal government must ensure the implementation of the long overdue tighter NOx and VOCs emission standards. In 1990, the government promised to limit car emissions of NOx to 0.25 grams/km and VOCs to 0.16 grams/km by 1994-95.

Recommendation 10
Road-user charges should be imposed to discourage commuters from driving in areas served by light rail or public transit. These charges could take the form of required transit passes (e.g., GO passes) to be displayed in vehicle windows. High fines with strict enforcement would ensure compliance.

Recommendation 11
The federal and provincial governments should consider the use of a carbon tax. Given the variations of carbon content in fuels, this tax would encourage the use of cleaner fuels. It would also encourage people to make greater use of public transportation. Compensation measures should be used, though, to eliminate the potential inequities that this kind of tax could bring.

Recommendation 12
All levels of government should use their procurement policies to show support for the use of cleaner fuels. More specifically, the province should adopt a goal of achieving a 10% share of natural gas in new light duty vehicles by 2005. The provincial and federal governments should also require the use of 10% ethanol blends in 100% of the auto stock (except natural gas and diesel vehicles) by 1995.

Recommendation 13
A surcharge should be applied to certain virgin materials used in cars, such as lead for lead acid batteries. This would reverse the current situation where primary lead is less expensive than secondary lead. The potential for reusing rubber in tires should also be assessed, and a tax applied to the use of virgin rubber.

Recommendation 14
Canadian car manufacturers should follow the example being set in Europe by designing cars for disassembly. This should include the labelling of all parts so they can be easily reused or recycled.

Recommendation 15
The federal and provincial governments should work with industry to take the most polluting cars off Ontario's roads. This removal program should also include the recycling of these older, inefficient cars.

Recommendation 16

The provincial government should press the federal government to amend the Federal Income Tax Act so that companies cannot deduct the cost of providing free or subsidized parking to their employees. The provincial government should amend the Commercial Concentration Tax so that exemptions are not provided to companies that offer free parking.

These measures should be complemented by incentives in the form of tax deductions to provide transit passes for employees, or to provide subsidized parking for High Occupancy Vehicles (HOVs).

Recommendation 17

Annual registration fees should be increased for second and third vehicles, especially in southern Ontario. This would provide revenue to the government to help pay for an inspection program, and would discourage multiple car ownership.

Recommendation 18

Public transportation should become the heart of Ontario's transportation policy. Emphasis should be placed on expanding the subway in Metropolitan Toronto and taking advantage of existing rail corridors for GO inter-urban service. Surface transit should be made more efficient through the use of dedicated lanes and signal priority systems.

Recommendation 19

In areas of lower population density, car and van pools should be encouraged. As well, demand-responsive operator-dispatched vans can be used if travel is frequent but not heavy enough to support a permanent bus route.

Recommendation 20

Bicycles are not just pleasure vehicles. Municipal governments should recognize the value of bicycles for commuting by creating safe bicycle paths. The TTC should provide more bicycle spaces at its stations and the public and private sector should encourage employees to bicycle to work by providing locking places and shower facilities.

Recommendation 21

Municipal governments should restrict the use of cars on some roads in city centres. This would make those areas more desirable for walking and shopping. People coming from outside the city centre would be encouraged to take public transit.

Recommendation 22

Instead of accommodating the growing use of the car by building new roads, the province and municipalities should focus on traffic management. Traffic calming involves the use of landscaping and low speed limits to discourage the use the car.

Recommendation 23

Travel on main roads should be made more efficient through the use of modern signal equipment. This would reduce car emissions due to unnecessary frequent starting and stopping.

Recommendation 24

With the proliferation of communications technology, substantial energy and emission savings can be realized by combining home and the workplace. Employers should encourage working from home whenever possible.

Recommendation 25

An education program should be launched by the provincial government to inform drivers of the car's impact on human health and the environment. A program similar to the drinking and driving campaign would be extremely effective in showing how much the car truly costs society.

Recommendation 26

Individuals should consider the hidden costs of the car when making decisions on lifestyle. Deliberately leaving the car at home one or two days a week would gradually reduce dependence on the car and would increase public transit ridership, thereby encouraging transit officials to improve their systems.

Acknowledgements

This report was prepared by David McRobert, Greg Hein, Alex Palimaka and Tija Luste. It could not have been completed without the generous assistance of many volunteers.

The project was conceived in August 1990 when David McRobert was contacted by Professor Beth Savan of the University of Toronto regarding potential research projects for her students. Mr. McRobert acted as the research coordinator for the project from September 1990 to April 1991.

Research was undertaken during this project by Tony Bastardi, Rita Corcoran, Susan Molnar, Alex Palimaka and Lisa Whittle -- five undergraduate students in Prof. Savan's course at Innis College. Pollution Probe is extremely grateful for the remarkable research undertaken by these students.

A 150-page report based on their work, titled "The True Cost of the Automobile" was submitted to Pollution Probe at the end of April 1991. Greg Hein, a researcher hired by Pollution Probe in May 1991, prepared an abridged version of that report. His draft served as the basis for this report. Alex Palimaka and Tony Bastardi, currently employed by the City of Toronto as researchers to elaborate and refine their original work, assisted in this task.

The authors wish to thank Bruce Lourie, Kathy Cooper and Dan Harvey for reviewing this report. Their comments have been invaluable. Thanks also go to Tija Luste, who was hired as a researcher to incorporate the reviewers' comments and do the final editing. Michael Schulman also helped with the editing.

Pollution Probe acknowledges the support of the Ontario Ministry of the Environment for the Environmental Youth Corps contracts which facilitated the hiring of Mr. Hein and Ms. Luste.

Much of the analysis in this report draws information from studies already available. Pollution Probe acknowledges the work of numerous researchers in the painstaking preparation of the original publications cited in the body of this report. The researchers who worked on this report also acknowledge the information and recommendations provided to them by staff and volunteers of many other organizations, including the Green Transportation Campaign (of which Pollution Probe is a member).

Any inaccuracies or mistakes in this report are the responsibility of the authors.

SECTION 1: INTRODUCTION

North Americans have fostered a reliance on the car unequalled by other societies. More than any other society, North Americans depend on the car for commuting to work, grocery shopping and basic travel. Roads, land-use planning, community design and public transit have all put the car first, with the result that a car is now considered by most to be a necessity of life.

This dependence has made the car an icon for North American society. Endless car styles, colours and names are available to suit any personality. The architecture of new homes reflects the prominence of the car, with large garages replacing porches on the fronts of houses. As well, North Americans are very protective of the supposed freedom offered by the car. Some even express their use of a car as a "right" not to be tampered with. This was demonstrated in Metro Toronto when proposals intended to speed up transit services on Metro roads were announced in March 1991. Many car drivers were adamantly opposed to any changes that would give buses and streetcars preferential treatment. One driver, opposed to the idea of having automatic green lights for streetcars, said, "I think they should take that idea to Russia".[1] At times, people seem to feel more strongly about their supposed "right" to drive than their right to vote.

There are numerous costs associated with this dependence on the car. These costs include direct government expenditures such as policing costs, health care costs for accident victims and increasing road construction and maintenance costs. Less obvious are many even greater costs which are borne by society. These hidden costs include the destruction of farmland, stress and loss of time due to traffic congestion, and ill health caused by car-related air pollution.

This report examines both the direct and hidden costs of the car in Ontario. In doing so, it raises a number of important public policy issues. Perhaps the most important issue is whether the

---

[1] Peter Small, "TTC Plan to Restrict Traffic Draws Some Motorist Approval", Toronto Star, 3 April 1991.

automobile is the most appropriate means of transportation in spite of its costs. If the costs of the car outweigh the benefits, then laws and policies should redirect transportation use away from the car. Decisions need to be made on how this should be achieved.

By looking at the various costs of the car it will be shown that drivers pay only part of the costs that arise from the use of the car; essentially, drivers are being subsidized to pollute.

This report concludes that the direct and hidden costs of the car are enormous and that they must be reduced. To this end, Pollution Probe has provided 26 recommendations aimed at individuals, business, industry and government. In areas of the province where public transit and bicycle commuting are feasible, there must be incentives to use them and disincentives to drive. Much of the potential for decreasing car use is in southern Ontario, particularly in the Greater Toronto Area where commuters account for a large portion of drivers. Thus, many of the recommendations are specific to that area. Throughout the province, and across the country, cars must be made more fuel efficient and exhaust emissions reduced. As well, land-use planning must not encourage a bias towards and reliance upon the car.

METHODOLOGY

The primary aim of this report is to uncover the hidden costs of the car.[2] This is done by compiling an inventory of the impacts of the car on all aspects of life. In Sections 2, 3, 4 and 5 the land-use, environmental, health and social costs of the car are identified. Within these four sections, a distinction is made between direct costs and hidden costs.

If a cost can be linked to a government expenditure, such as annual budgeted outlays for road construction and maintenance, it is characterized as direct. A cost is also labelled as direct if it is

---

[2] This study does not consider the impact of the transportation sector as a whole. Instead, it tries to focus on the use of cars or "private passenger vehicles". Included in this category are privately owned cars, light duty trucks and vans used to transport passengers; not included are taxis and rental cars. Emission statistics do not include large fleets of cars owned by corporations and governments.

in the form of one-time government spending, such as for the Hagersville tire fire cleanup. A hidden cost is defined as a cost which is not linked to a government expenditure. For example, a hidden cost may be borne by an individual in the form of ill health, or by future generations in the form of a premature lack of natural resources.

This report provides estimates for some of the hidden costs of the car, while acknowledging that many costs are unquantifiable. For example, it is difficult to place a value on urban green-spaces, travel time, respiratory problems, or life itself. The figures cited in this report are preliminary estimates, designed to indicate the extent of the hidden costs of the car. The authors recognize that a true cradle-to-grave cost of the car is beyond the scope of this report, mostly due to the unavailability of sufficiently disaggregated statistics.

Ontario's economic dependence on the car is discussed in Section 6. This dependence results in government car-related expenditures exceeding car-related revenue, with the implication that the government subsidizes drivers. The bias towards the car is a barrier to encouraging alternative modes of transportation. Section 7 calculates a total estimated cost of the car to society and lists all the various ways in which the car impacts society.

This report draws primarily on Ontario data. Where information was unavailable, American or European studies were often used. Several techniques were used to gather information. Most information was collected from published research reports or articles describing such research. In addition, numerous in-person and telephone interviews were conducted with government and industry officials.

Once the data were collected, the figures were standardized and adjusted for inflation. For the sake of simplicity, all monetary figures (unless otherwise stated) were converted into 1990 dollars using the consumer price index (CPI) to account for inflation.

SECTION 2: LAND-USE COSTS

Ontario's dependence on the car is most apparent in southern Ontario, where multi-lane highways connect large urban centres like Metro Toronto and Hamilton to their many suburbs. Every day, at the same times of the morning and late afternoon, southern Ontario's highways become overloaded with cars -- many having only one or two passengers. In addition, the distances that people are willing to commute have reached absurd levels. For example, many people commute every day from Barrie, 100 km from downtown Toronto!

The story of the car and land-use is a relatively simple one. At the same time Canadians were building much of the nation's housing and infrastructure, the car was enjoying a popularity boom, and fuel was relatively cheap. As populations increased, so did the number of cars, roads and supporting structures like parking lots and service stations. Figure 1 shows the growth in the number of vehicles in Ontario from 1970 to 1986. By 1986, Canadians owned 11.5 million cars, while Ontario residents owned roughly 4 million cars.[3] The province's infrastructure had fast become car-centred -- more and more land-use planning and transportation planning was based on the needs of a society dependent on cars.

The widespread use of the car has allowed for an unprecedented degree of reorganization of the way people, institutions and industries used space. More people could choose to live in the suburbs or even adjacent rural areas where housing was comparatively cheaper, but still work in cities or towns. Thus, while the population of Metro Toronto has remained about the same for the past ten years, the outlying regions have undergone tremendous growth. This urban sprawl has put heavy demands on the province's road system. Existing highways have been widened and new ones have been built to meet these demands.

---

[3] Pollution Probe, et al, The Canadian Green Consumer Guide (Toronto: McClelland & Stewart, 1991).

Figure 1. Number of Vehicles in Ontario (1970-1986)

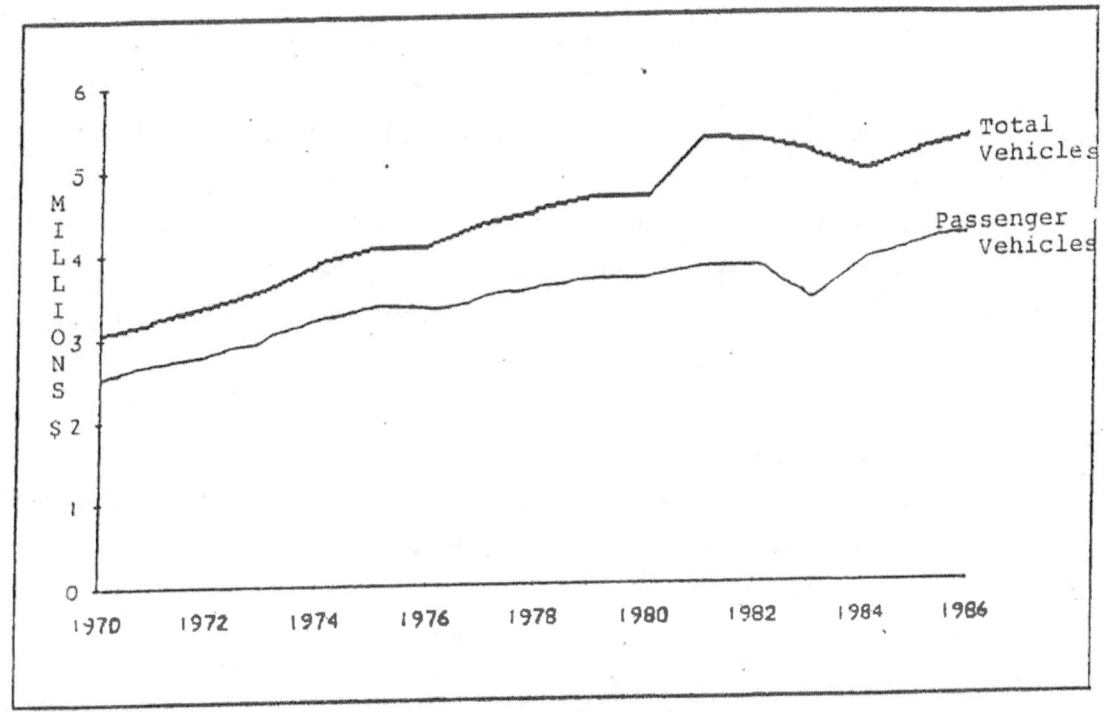

Sources : Statistics Canada, Road Registrations: 1964-80;
Statistics Canada, Canada Year Book 1990;
Sectoral and Regional Branch of Ontario Ministry
of Treasury and Economics

5

By definition, suburbs have lower population densities than Metropolitan cores. Figure 2 shows these differences in densities in the Greater Toronto Area (GTA). The problem this poses is that a population residing in a low-density suburb is more difficult to serve efficiently with public transportation. The level of service offered in some low density areas does not provide an adequate incentive for people to leave their cars at home.

As a result, residents in low density areas rely primarily on the private automobile for transportation needs. Figure 3 shows that there is a strong correlation between levels of urban density and the use of private transportation.[4] Toronto's location on the graph shows that relative to our density, our urban transit systems are used slightly more often than in major American or Australian cities, but are underutilized relative to major European and Asian cities. In sum, this research shows that the infrastructures of Canada, the United States and Australia favour the use of the car, and are biased against the use of other more efficient modes of transportation.

Lastly, there are indications that a reliance on the car may be accelerating rapidly, especially on the outskirts of Metropolitan Toronto. As one US expert recently stated: "When I visited Toronto in 1989 I came on a pilgrimage to a city that still had great public transit; this time [in 1991] I was shocked by how much it felt like an automobile city".[5]

---

[4] P. Newman and J. Kenworthy, Cities and Automobile Dependence (Sydney: Gower Technical, 1989). Hereinafter: Newman & Kenworthy, Cities.

[5] C. Hume, "U.S. Expert Fears Cars Will Ruin Amazing Metro", Toronto Star, 1 May 1991, A1-2.

Figure 2. Population Densities of the Greater Toronto Area and
Metro Toronto Municipalities (people/hectare)

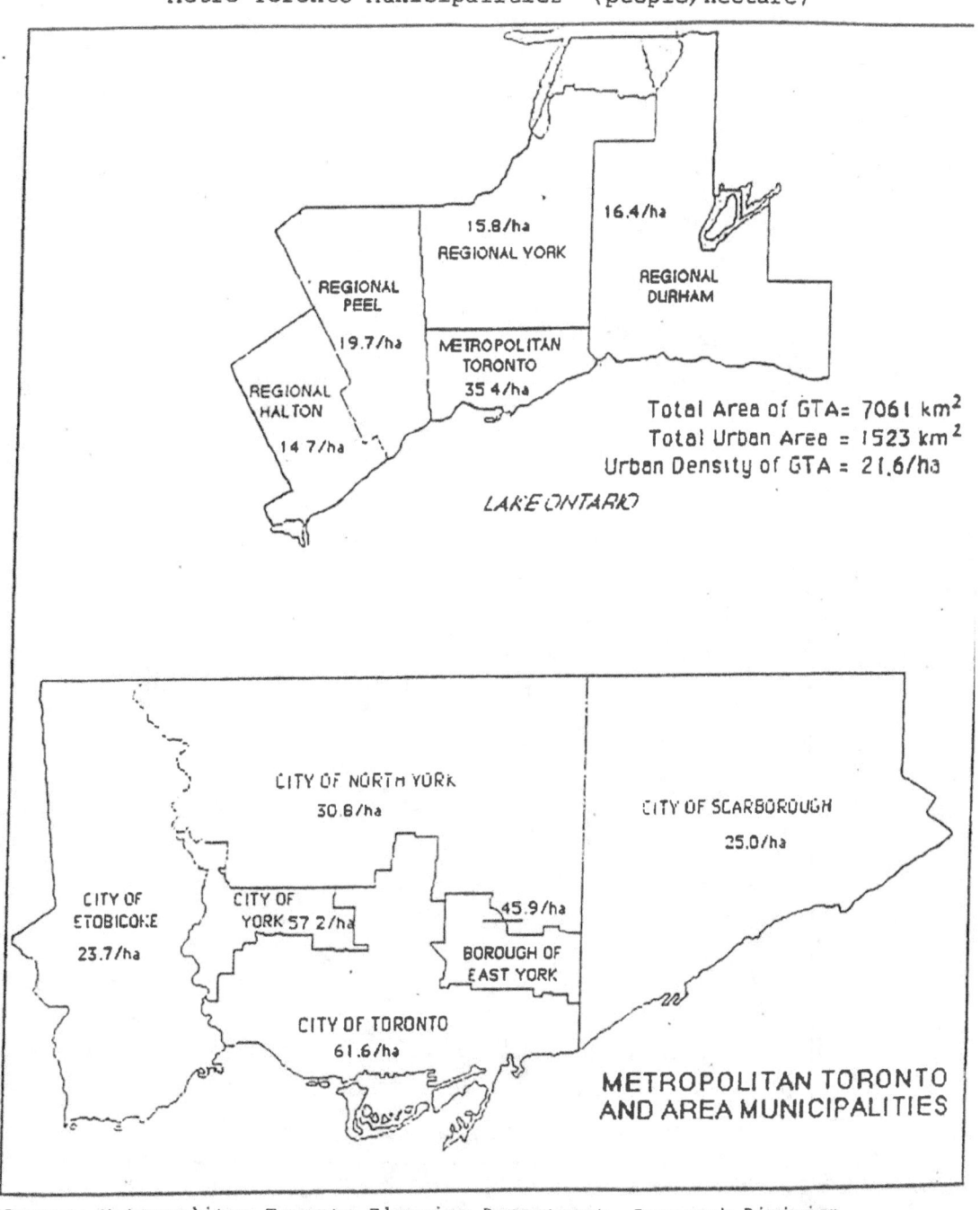

Total Area of GTA = 7061 km^2
Total Urban Area = 1523 km^2
Urban Density of GTA = 21.6/ha

Source: Metropolitan Toronto Planning Department, Research Division
Metropolitan Toronto Key Facts 1990

FIGURE 3. Percentage of Workers Using Private Transport Versus Urban Density in Major Cities

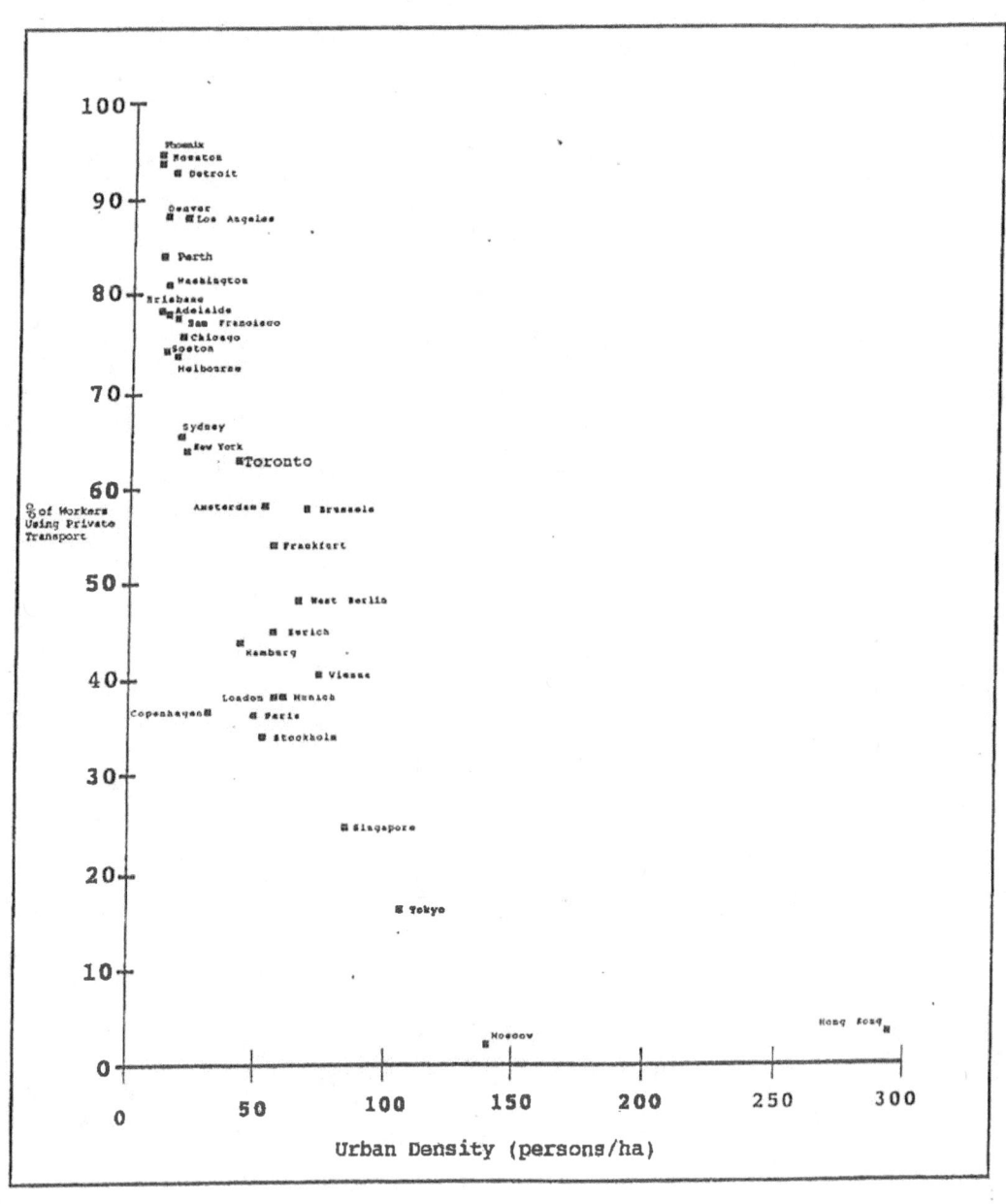

Sour   wman & Kenworthy (1989).

DIRECT COSTS

1) Highway Expenditures.

For the fiscal year 1989-90, the cost of building and maintaining provincial highways was $798 million.[6] The cost of highway construction and repair is even more staggering when federal and municipal expenditures are included. In 1988, total government spending on Canada's road infrastructure was in excess of $5.3 billion.[7] Of the total spent, $1.9 billion was allocated to Ontario. These funds were directed towards the construction and maintenance of highways, roads and bridges.

As well, a considerable portion of the province's debt can be attributed to spending on roads. A submission to the Standing Committee of the Ontario Legislature on Finance and Economic Affairs presented by the Ontario Chapter of Transport 2000 suggests that the interest in fiscal year 1989-90 on previous car-related deficits was $1,173 million.[8]

It is also crucial to consider the increasing share of highway spending that goes towards repair and maintenance. Since 1978, the cost of repairing Ontario's roads has risen considerably. As the number of commuters and the number of highways increase, more funding will be required for maintenance alone.

HIDDEN COSTS

1) Destruction of Agricultural Land and Urban Green-space.

The car has had a great impact on Ontario's agricultural land. As more land is used for roads, parking lots, garages, car washes and car dealerships, less is available for agricultural activity. Moreover, much of the land in danger is Ontario's prime farmland. About one-half of

---

[6] Henry Bird, Maintenance Budget Comptroller, Ontario Ministry of Transportation, personal communication to Greg Hein (1991).

[7] Statistics Canada, Canada Year Book (Ottawa: Statistics Canada, 1989).

[8] Ibid.

the first-class agricultural land in Canada lies within 80 kilometres of Canada's 20 largest cities. Pollution Probe researchers estimate that successive Ontario governments have paved over a million hectares of land to construct the 160,000 kilometres of highways in the province.[9] Assuming a conservative price of $1,000/hectare,[10] this land would be worth over $1 billion dollars at current market value. In response to concern about urban sprawl, Metro Toronto Council recently called on the province to freeze development on all agricultural land in the GTA for a full year.[11]

Demand for resources like crushed stone, or aggregate, needed by the construction industry is another pressure on agricultural land and other rural lands which may be environmentally sensitive. Environmentalists have sought changes to legislation regarding the development of these lands in Ontario, but much more remains to be done.[12]

Recommendations

1. The province's Planning Act should be amended. Future planning should be based on five principles: (i) to intensify and concentrate development in areas that are already built up; (ii) to adopt minimum residential densities in developing areas; (iii) to limit office development to sites well served by public transit; (iv) to protect important farmland and natural areas; (v) to require any new development, especially outside the Greater Toronto Area, to include requirements for public transportation.

2. The proposed community of Seaton should not be built. It would be built on valuable farmland and many of its residents would work and shop in Toronto, making it another "bedroom" community.

---

[9] Pollution Probe, "Greening Canada's Passenger Transportation System", brief presented to the Royal Commission on National Passenger Transportation (July 1990), 19-20.

[10] Prices for land vary across Ontario, depending on the quality of land and the location. Prime agricultural land in southern Ontario can cost up to $3,500/ha.

[11] J. Byers, "Development freeze urged for farmland", Toronto Star, 6 June 1991, A12.

[12] See Ontario Environment Network, Sustainability As If We Mean It, position paper prepared for the Ontario Roundtable on the Environment and the Economy (April 1991).

The car also has a negative impact on the availability of land for urban green space. With the ever-present pressures to create more parking space, small and large green spaces in Metro Toronto and other Ontario cities are often sacrificed. It has been estimated that parking a single car at home, the office, and the shopping mall requires on average 4,000 square feet of asphalt.[13] Worldwide, it is estimated that at least a third of an average city's land is devoted to roads, parking lots, and other elements of the car infrastructure.[14]

Lastly, the disposal and temporary storage of discarded cars and their component parts has a negative impact on land use. The junking of old cars and car parts takes up valuable space. Moreover, the land around these dump sites has limited use, for aesthetic and environmental reasons.[15]

2) Excessive Energy Consumption.

Urban sprawl is costly. Longer distances between the workplace and home result in higher volumes of traffic in the mornings and evenings. This leads to excessive fuel use, partly because of the longer distances and partly because fuel is wasted in traffic jams. The City's Planning and Development Department has determined that for every 1,000 housing units built in downtown Toronto, total inbound car trips could be reduced by about 1,200 in the morning peak period.[16] Denser development within the city centre, particularly in Toronto, would result in large reductions in emissions.

---

[13] Michael Renner, Rethinking the Role of the Automobile, Worldwatch Paper #84 (1988).

[14] Ibid.

[15] The environmental impacts of disposal are discussed in Section 3 of this report.

[16] Healthy City Office, City of Toronto & the Technical Working Group on Traffic Calming and Vehicle Emission Reduction, Evaluating the Role of the Automobile: A Municipal Strategy (September 1991), 103. Hereinafter: Healthy City Office, Evaluating the Role of the Automobile.

In their landmark study, Newman and Kenworthy document the relationship between gas use and urban density: when population densities are high, less gas is used.[17] As Figure 4 shows, Newman and Kenworthy have found great variations in per capita gasoline use among different cities. For example, they found that Toronto consumes about one and a half times as much as major European cities, and five times as much as Singapore, Tokyo or Hong kong.

Recommendations

3. In order to encourage land-use intensification, the province and City of Toronto should ensure that the Railway Lands are developed for residential units. Together with other new central area neighbourhoods and the "Main Streets" initiative, these residential areas will result in great energy savings and emission reductions.

4. Individuals should consider the environmental consequences of where and in what type of housing they choose to live. A conscious decision to live in already built up areas or to live in higher density housing is the best way to prevent urban sprawl.

---

[17] Newman and Kenworthy, Cities, op. cit.

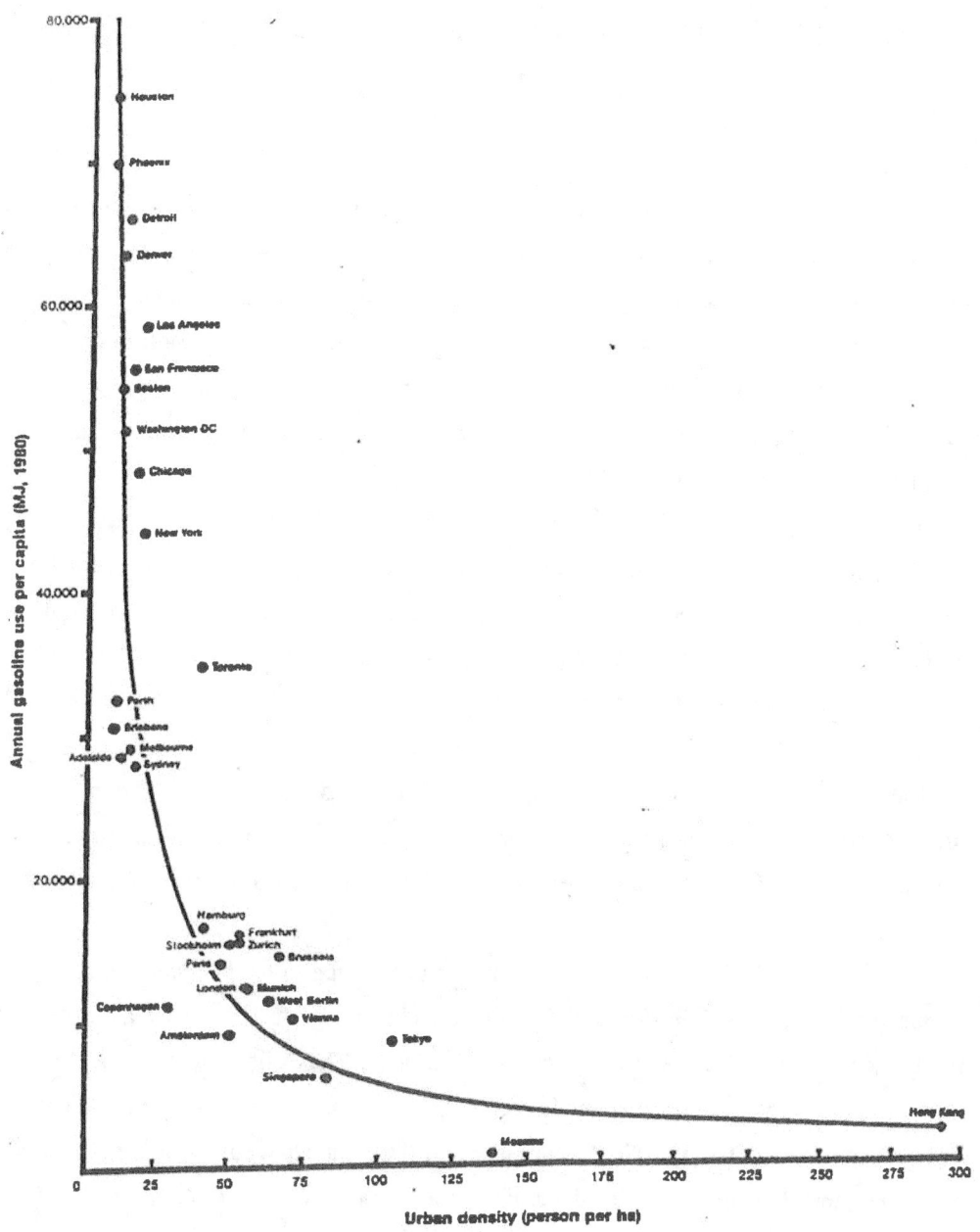

Figure 4 .   Gasoline use per capita versus urban density (1980).

Source: Newman & Kenworthy,

13

SECTION 3: ENVIRONMENTAL COSTS

DIRECT COSTS:

1) Government Spending on the Environment.

Both the federal and the provincial governments spend billions of dollars annually trying to control pollution. This money is spent monitoring polluting industries, enforcing emission standards, managing waste streams, and cleaning up the environment after damage has occurred. By far the most spending is on cleanup, and a large percentage of that is attributable to the automobile. For example, while the entire Ontario Ministry of the Environment budget for 1990-91 is $775 million, it has been estimated that the Hagersville tire fire alone will cost the government $50 million between 1990 and 1992.

Comparatively speaking, spending on the environment represents very little of total government spending. In 1989-90, the Ontario Ministry of the Environment's budget made up just over 1% of the Ontario budget. Environment Canada's budget for 1987-88 was $774 million, which represents 0.84% of total spending for that year.

The levels of government spending on the environment are significant for two reasons. First, given the widespread and persistent impact of the car and its supporting industries, it is inevitable that a significant portion of spending to control pollution can be attributed to the car.

Second, the level of spending is significant when compared to the budgets of other departments. The Ontario Ministry of Transportation's budget is much greater than the Ministry of the Environment's. Macdonald writes in his recent book, The Politics of Pollution, that "Ontario gives priority, expressed in public spending, to transportation over four times greater than that given to environmental protection".[18] Simply put, the cumulative cost of water pollution, acidification, ground-level ozone, global warming, and ozone depletion are not accounted for in current levels of government spending.

---

[18] Macdonald, Doug, The Politics of Pollution (Toronto: McClelland & Stewart, 1991).

14

HIDDEN COSTS

1) Mining.

Mining is energy intensive. In 1988, it ranked fifth in energy use out of all industrial sectors in Ontario, using 50 terajoules of energy.[19] This results in the depletion of non-renewable resources. Another environmental problem frequently associated with mining is acid mine drainage or acid runoff. The pH level of mine wastewater is often very low, and the runoff carries dissolved heavy metals. A report co-authored by the Mining Association of Canada found that "acid mine drainage can pose a threat to human health and to the environment".[20]

The Ontario government has recently acknowledged that past mining has "left a significant legacy of abandoned mines and tailing sites."[21] Ontario has about 3,000 abandoned mine sites, with about 80 of these posing some degree of hazard to the environment and human health. Cost estimates to return these lands to "acceptable form" are on the order of $3 billion over a 15-year period.[22]

Mining also contributes to air pollution. According to one report prepared by Environment Canada in 1984, the mining of metals accounts for 8.3% of total particulate emissions and 3.4% of total sulphur oxide emissions.[23] Mining for metals to produce cars makes up a small portion of total mining, but it can pose serious localized environmental problems in rural areas.

---

[19] Ontario Global Warming Coalition, Degrees of Change: Steps Towards an Ontario Global Warming Strategy, Philip Jessup, et al, eds., prepared for the Ontario Ministry of Energy and Ontario Ministry of the Environment (June 1991), 54. Tera = trillion. Hereinafter: OGWC, Degrees of Change.

[20] Tom Spears, "Waste Cleanup Will Need $3 Billion", Ottawa Citizen, 25 October 1990.

[21] Ontario Roundtable on Environment and Economy, "Energy and Minerals Task Force Consultation Document" (May 1991).

[22] Ibid.

[23] Environment Canada, Emission Trends of Common Air Contaminants in Canada: 1970-1980 (1984). Hereinafter: Environment Canada, Emission Trends.

In addition to the metals used to make cars and bridges, rocks and sand are extracted to build roads. Rock quarries scar the landscape and destroy habitat. More than 64% of Canada's production from quarries and sand pits goes into road beds and surfaces.[24]

2) Metal Smelting.

According to Statistics Canada, the auto industry uses 13.8% of all metal alloys produced in Canada.[25] The smelting of metals has an impact on both water resources and air quality. Given that the car and its supporting industries use about 18% of all steel in Canada, the car is responsible for a large amount of water and air pollution from smelters.

Ontario's four iron and steel plants discharge huge amounts of toxins into Ontario waters each year. For example, in 1988 45 tonnes of cyanide, 80,000 tonnes of phenolics and 1,800 tonnes of ammonia were discharged by these plants.[26]

In terms of air pollution, metal smelting contributes 5.6% of total particulates and 45% of sulphur oxide emissions in Canada.[27] The iron and steel industry is responsible for 15% of all CO_2 emissions in Ontario.[28] The steel smelting industry uses coke, an inefficient energy source, for a lot of its energy. A report prepared by the Ontario Global Warming Coalition states that the use of coke by the steel industry accounts for almost 9% of Ontario's total CO_2 emissions.[29] In addition, sulphur from the smelting process contributes to acid rain.

---

[24] Statistics Canada, Catalogue 26-225 Quarries and Sand Pits (1985).

[25] Statistics Canada, Catalogue 41-001 Primary Iron and Steel (December 1989).

[26] Ontario Ministry of the Environment, Report on the 1988 Industrial Direct Discharges in Ontario (1989).

[27] Environment Canada, Emission Trends, op. cit.

[28] OGWC, Degrees of Change, op. cit.

[29] Ibid, 70.

3) Energy Use.

To manufacture a car, including all the materials, assembly and maintenance, 5,600 kwh in electricity and the equivalent of 19,700 kwh in fossil fuels are needed. The total amount of electricity used to manufacture cars in Canada is about 11% of publicly generated electricity.[30]

The daily use of cars also requires huge amounts of energy. In Canada, 28.8% of energy consumed is for transportation.[31] A comparison of transportation modes reveals the inefficiency of the car: while a commuter train carrying 80 passengers requires roughly 710 British thermal units (BTUs) of energy per passenger mile, a car carrying one person one mile requires 7,380 BTUs.[32]

The energy demands related to road building and car manufacturing and use are met through oil consumption, hydro-electricity and the burning of fossil fuels. All of these activities have important environmental impacts, some of which are described in other sections of this report.

---

[30] Statistics Canada, Catalogue 57-208, Consumption of Purchased Fuel and Electricity: 1984 (1987). This includes the car's share of petroleum refining.

[31] Statistics Canada, Catalogue 57-003, Passenger Car Fuel Consumption Survey (1988).

[32] Marcia Lowe, "Out of the Car, Into the Future", World Watch (November/December 1990) 21.

4) Petroleum Industry.

Private vehicle gasoline use accounts for 28% of the petroleum industry refined product output, while car-related lubricants and petrochemical products account for an additional 3.1%. Thus, the car uses approximately 31% of the petroleum industry's total refined output.[33] This makes the car accountable for a large portion of petroleum industry-related pollution.

In the first stage of the petroleum cycle, the disposal of toxic drilling fluid contaminates surrounding vegetation and soil. As well, the refining of petroleum and the production of chemicals used to make the car's component parts have a serious impact on Ontario's water resources. Ontario's seven petroleum refineries discharge thousands of tonnes of toxins into rivers and lakes. In 1988-89, they discharged 261 kg of benzene, 3,766 kg of chromium and 34 kg of

---

[33] For information on calculations, see A. Palimaka and A. Bastardi, report to the City of Toronto Environmental Advisory Committee, forthcoming.

phenol.[34] Petroleum refineries are not the only car-related industries discharging toxins into Ontario waters. Other examples of water contamination include: the discharging of nitrosamine into Elmira's water supply by Uniroyal;[35] the dumping of ethylbenzene, toluene, styrene, and dichlorobenzene into the St. Clair River by Dow Chemical;[36] and the discharging of PCBs from Goodyear's engine belt plant into Owen Sound.[37]

In terms of air pollution, crude oil production and petroleum refining result in the release of 2.4% of total industrial sulphur oxide emissions and 8.6% of total industrial hydrocarbon emissions in Canada.[38] While emission standards do exist, they are sometimes breached. For instance, at least once in the fall of 1990, Petro-Canada's Oakville refinery violated Ontario's standard for sulphide emissions. On September 14, emissions of reduced sulphides topped 211 ppb -- nearly eight times the provincial standard of 27 ppb.[39]

The transportation of oil within Canada also has a negative impact on the environment. In Ontario, 95% of the oil consumed comes from western Canada via the Interprovincial Pipe Line System.[40] The transportation of oil along this line affects the ecosystems it passes through; it triggers mud flows, causes soil erosion, and disturbs wildlife migration patterns.

---

[34] Ontario Ministry of the Environment, Second Report on the Monitoring Data for the Petroleum Refining Sector, (1990).

[35] "Uniroyal Wants to Dump More Waste on This Community, But Still Refuses to Accept Responsibility for Past Mess", Elmira Independent, 5 November 1990.

[36] Gary Rennie, "Grier Blasts Dow Over Spills", Windsor Star, 7 November 1990.

[37] "Goodyear Closes in Owen Sound", Whig Standard, 24 September 1990.

[38] Environment Canada, Emission Trends, op. cit.

[39] Shaun Herron, "Refinery Under Investigation Over Sulphur Gas Emission", Hamilton Spectator, 10 October 1990. The Oakville refinery was also under investigation for producing gasoline which emits illegal amounts of hydrocarbons into the air when burned.

[40] Ontario Ministry of Energy, Ontario Energy Review (1990).

Recent history has shown, though, that the transportation of oil and gas by ship is much more potentially dangerous. There are dozens of examples of large and small spills, like the Exxon Valdez spill, and the recent spill of 162,000 litres of fuel into Ontario's Georgian Bay.[41] Regardless of size, the impact can be devastating. The US EPA has estimated that one quart of oil can contaminate and make undrinkable 250,000 gallons of drinking water, and that same quart can produce a thin film two acres wide on the surface of an ocean, a lake or canal.[42]

A study undertaken on behalf of the Federal government in 1990, Protecting Our Waters, investigated Canada's ability to cope with major spills. It concluded that the consequences of a major spill in the Great Lakes would likely be devastating for wildlife and the drinking water of 24 million people.[43] Protecting Our Waters reports that almost 13 million tonnes of petroleum and other hazardous products are shipped annually in the Great Lakes.

Finally, oil fires pose a serious environmental threat. The US National Science Foundation has estimated that 1 to 2 million tons of carbon dioxide have been released into the atmosphere daily by the Kuwaiti fires.[44] Although Ontario does not import oil from Kuwait, the oil fires in Kuwait represent a serious threat to the world's atmosphere and Ontario's contribution to the universal dependence on oil should not be ignored.

5) Air Pollutants.

Cars emit pollutants through their exhausts and through the deterioration of their component parts. The main pollutants emitted through exhaust fumes are carbon monoxide, hydrocarbons, nitrogen oxides, carbon dioxide and, to a lesser extent, sulphur dioxide. Air conditioning units in

---

[41] Peter Gorrie, "Lake Fuel Spill Just a Warning", Toronto Star, 20 May 1991.

[42] See Saab, "How to Maintain Your Car and Environmental Conscience" (1991).

[43] John Flanders, "Big Spill Could Devastate Great Lakes: New Report", Hamilton Spectator, 3 November 1990.

[44] J. George & B. Blackwelder, "Oil Fires: A Mideast Chernobyl?", Toronto Star, 10 July 1991.

many cars leak chlorofluorocarbons (CFCs). Heavy metals are also emitted by the automobile. These various emissions contribute to acidification, elevated levels of ground level ozone, global warming and ozone depletion.

a) SOx, NOx and Acidification.

Acid rain is primarily caused by emissions of sulphur dioxide and nitrogen oxides; both are emitted by cars and other industrial sources. The private passenger car is responsible for approximately 9.7% of human-induced SOx emissions and 17.7 % of human-induced NOx emissions[45], either through tail-pipe emissions or car-related industrial smokestack emissions. Once released into the atmosphere, these substances are carried long distances by the prevailing winds, and return to earth in the form of acid rain. In addition, acid compounds released from melting snow contribute to spring "acid shock" in some areas of eastern Canada.[46] When the environment cannot neutralize the acid, significant damage to ecosystems occurs.

The potential impact of acid rain is great -- 43% of Canada's land area is sensitive to acidic deposition.[47] Acidification has already had an impact on the terrestrial environment. Approximately 15 million hectares of hardwood and mixed wood forests in eastern Canada are at risk.[48] Fifty-five percent of eastern Canada's forests, which generate $14 billion worth of forest products, as well as 84% of the most productive agricultural land, annually receive more than the

---

[45] A. Palimaka and A. Bastardi, report to the City of Toronto Environmental Advisory Committee, forthcoming.

[46] Canadian Council of Ministers of the Environment, Management Plan for NOx and VOCs, Phase 1 (November 1990). Hereinafter: CCME, Management Plan.

[47] Federal/Provincial Research and Monitoring Coordinating Committee, The 1990 Canadian Long-Range Transport of Air Pollutants and Acid Deposition Assessment Report, Part I (1990). Hereinafter: RMCC, Long-Range Transport.

[48] Ibid.

21

acceptable level of acid rain.[49] Studies in southern Ontario indicate that acidification has already played a significant role in the decline of sugar maples.[50]

Lakes are also damaged by acid rain. Survey data have shown that in eastern Canada there are more than 31,000 acidic lakes greater than 0.18 hectares in size; 14,000 of these are greater than one hectare in size.[51]

In the North, there is the lesser known problem of "Arctic haze". In the 1950s, airplane pilots were the first to notice that mountains and coastlines were sometimes obscured by particles in the atmosphere. During the 1970s, scientists discovered that the haze is actually air pollution which has travelled great distances from industrialized areas.[52] The haze consists mainly of fine droplets of sulphuric acid. Besides reducing visibility, this haze is likely to contribute to climate warming; it could increase the average temperature by up to 2 degrees Celsius during the months of March, April and May.[53]

In sum, acid rain has a negative impact on forestry, water resources, the North and agriculture. Total damage due to acidification in Canada was estimated to be about $250 million per year in 1985.[54] Private passenger vehicle-related emissions of sulphur oxides and nitrogen oxides equal approximately 9.7% and 17.7%, respectively, of total emissions. Given this, and

---

[49] Transport Canada, A Plan to Identify and Assess Emission Reduction Opportunities from Transportation, Industrial Engines, and Motor Fuels (1989).

[50] D. Mclaughlin, et al, Sugar Maple Decline in Ontario, (Ministry of the Environment, 1987).

[51] RMCC, Long-Range Transport, op. cit.

[52] Environment Canada, Arctic Haze: Visible Air Pollution (1989).

[53] Ibid.

[54] John McCormick, Acid Earth: The Global Threat of Acid Pollution (London: Earthscan and IIED, 1985). This is a conservative estimate. Some estimates value damage due to acid rain at about $1 billion (Statistics Canada).

assuming that sulphur oxides account for 60% of acid rain and nitrogen oxides for 40%, car-related emissions account for 13% of acid rain.[55] Thus, the car is responsible for about $32.5 million damage attributable to acidification each year in Canada. Ontario's share of this would be about $13 million.

b) NOx, VOCs and Ground Level Ozone.

In the presence of sunlight, volatile organic compounds (VOCs, also called hydrocarbons) catalyze reactions between nitrogen oxides and oxygen to produce ground level ozone. Benzene, toluene, ethylene and xylene are all VOCs emitted in the exhaust of cars. The majority of car trips in Ontario are made in the Windsor-Quebec City corridor. Cars and light duty trucks emit 34% of total NOx and 31% of total VOCs in the corridor.[56] In the Greater Toronto Area, personal car use on a typical workday emits roughly 60 tonnes of nitrogen oxides and 100 tonnes of volatile organic compounds.[57]

When compared to other modes of transportation, the car's capacity to pollute is clearly superior. Emissions of hydrocarbons and nitrogen oxides for various modes are shown in Table 1.[58]

---

[55] Neville Reid (Ontario MOE, Supervisor for the Air Quality Branch), personal communication to Pollution Probe, 1991.

[56] CCME, Management Plan, op. cit., 144-145.

[57] The Green Transportation Campaign, Greening Ontario's Transportation: A Public Campaign (1991). Hereinafter: GTC, Greening Ontario's Transportation.

[58] Marcia Lowe, "Out of the Car, Into the Future", op. cit.

**Table 1: VOCs and NOx Emissions for Different Modes of Transport
(grams/100 passenger miles)**

Mode	Emissions of VOCs	Emissions of NOx
Light rail	0.4	69
Transit buses	20	154
Car with 3 people	70	69
Car with one person	209	206

While ozone is needed in the stratosphere to filter ultraviolet radiation, it is harmful when present at ground levels. Researchers have linked elevated ozone levels to damage to forests and crops. Damage to vegetation is usually in the form of foliar injury which reduces productivity. Comparative studies of agricultural land with different levels of ozone exposure have shown that reduction of yields ranges from 1 to 20%.[59] For example, ozone is reported to reduce soybean, cotton, and other crop yields by 5 to 10%.[60] Studies have shown that the growth of vegetables is negatively affected by exposure to 25 ppb ozone, which is startling given that levels of ozone in the Windsor-Quebec corridor can peak at 160 ppb during the summer months.[61]

This loss of crops has serious economic implications. In Ontario, crop damage resulting from elevated levels of ozone is estimated at up to $70 million per year.[62] Given that car emissions are responsible for at least 31% of VOCs and 17.7% of NOx, it is estimated that at least 20% of ozone damage can be attributed to the private passenger vehicle, or up to $14 million crop

---

[59] CCME, Management Plan, op. cit., 8-9.

[60] Ibid.

[61] Ibid.

[62] RMCC, Long-Range Transport, op. cit.

damage each year. Ozone also affects the growth rates of trees. Exposure to ozone can lead to increased susceptibility to diseases and increased mortality of individual trees.[63] In eastern North America, ozone has been linked to the decline of red spruce, yellow pine and sugar maple.[64]

Recommendations

9. The federal government must ensure the implementation of the long overdue tighter NOx and VOCs emission standards. In 1990, the government promised to limit car emissions of NOx to 0.25 grams/km and VOCs to 0.16 grams/km by 1994-95.

10. Road-user charges should be imposed to discourage commuters from driving in areas served by light rail or public transit. These charges could take the form of required transit passes (e.g., GO passes) to be displayed in vehicle windows. High fines with strict enforcement would ensure compliance.

---

c) **Carbon Dioxide, CFCs, Ozone and Global Warming.**

The relative shares of human-induced greenhouse emissions are shown in Table 2.[65]

Table 2: Contributions of Greenhouse Gases to Global Warming

Carbon dioxide	55%
Methane	15%
CFCs	24%
Nitrous oxide	6%
TOTAL	100%

Motor vehicles are responsible for about 16% of the total human contribution to the greenhouse effect.[66]

---

[63] Ibid., 8-9.

[64] R. Friedman, et al, Urban Ozone and the Clean Air Act, Office of Technology Assessment (1988).

[65] Leggett, Jeremy, "The Nature of the Greenhouse Threat", Global Warming: The Greenpeace Report (1990).

[66] A. Palimaka and A. Bastardi, report to the City of Toronto Environmental Advisory Committee, forthcoming.

Private passenger vehicle emissions account for about 13% of all human releases of carbon dioxide,[67] while car-related industries contribute approximately another 5%.[68] Personal car use on a typical weekday in the Greater Toronto Area emits roughly 17,000 tonnes of carbon dioxide.[69]

Increased carbon dioxide concentrations in the atmosphere are suspected to be the primary cause of increased global temperatures. CFCs are the second most significant greenhouse gas. Some car air conditioners leak CFCs. The EPA estimates that CFCs in cars alone account for as much as 25% of CFC use in the US.[70]

Although there are still areas of uncertainty, most scientists agree on the range of possible consequences of increases in the amount of greenhouse gases.[71] There is general agreement that the global temperature will rise between 1.5 and 4.5 degrees Celsius in the next 50 to 75 years. This warming will profoundly change climate patterns.

Changes in wind and precipitation patterns will affect agricultural growing potentials. Increased temperatures in North America would greatly affect agricultural productivity; the unusual heat in 1988 was enough to reduce the North American grain crop by about 30%.[72] It is estimated that an increase in the average temperature of 3-4 degrees Celsius, accompanied by

---

[67] OGWC, Degrees of Change, op. cit.

[68] Ibid.; Statistics Canada, Catalogue 57-208, op. cit.

[69] GTC, Greening Ontario's Transportation, op. cit.

[70] John Elkington, et al, The Green Consumer (New York: Penguin, 1990), 72. Hereinafter: Elkington, The Green Consumer.

[71] James Bruce, "Myths and Realities of Global Climate Change", Ecodecision (1991) Vol. 1(1).

[72] George Woodwell, "The Effects of Global Warming", Global Warming: The Greenpeace Report, J. Leggett, ed. (New York: Oxford University Press, 1990), 125.

reduced soil moisture, will decrease yields of spring wheat in Canada by about 19%.[73] Problems with disease and pests will also increase.

The potential for massive flooding is a very real one. All land presently one metre above sea level will likely be flooded by the year 2100.[74] These changes in water levels and resources will affect all parts of the world. At greatest risk are those areas already arid and marginal, like deserts or semi-deserts. In Canada, built-up coastal areas are vulnerable to a rise in the sea level. One expert, Stokoe, projects losses of several hundred million dollars in Atlantic Canada for each of the following categories: urban waterfront land, buildings, breakwaters, bridges and causeways, roads and railways, fish processing plants and wharves.[75] Meanwhile, lake levels are expected to drop. Sanderson estimates that average annual costs to Canadian Great Lakes shipping companies from reduced lake levels may increase by about 30%.[76]

Climate changes will also have more direct effects on specific industries. For example, it has been projected that a doubling of carbon dioxide could eliminate the downhill ski season in the South Georgian Bay Region.[77] That would result in a loss of $36.6 million annually in skier spending, and a $12.8 million drop in spending in Collingwood.

It is likely that many species would be unable to adapt to rapid climate change. Some

---

[73] Intergovernmental Panel on Climate Change, Potential Impacts of Climate Change (1990), 2-14. Hereinafter: IPCC, Potential Impacts.

[74] Ibid., 6.

[75] Peter Stokoe, Socio-economic Assessment of the Physical and Ecological Impacts of Climate Change on the Marine Environment of the Atlantic Region of Canada, Environment Canada (1988).

[76] Marie Sanderson, "Implications of Climatic Change for Navigation and Power Generation in the Great Lakes", Environment Canada (1987).

[77] G. Wall, "Implications of Climatic Change for Tourism and Recreation in Ontario", Environment Canada (1988).

27

predict that entire ecosystems, such as boreal forests and coral reefs, could be lost.[78] The IPCC's Working Group II believes that the social and economic consequences of climate changes will be especially significant for those societies dependent on the land for their daily welfare.[79] Although it is difficult, if not impossible, to quantify all of the potential costs of global warming, it is clear that the magnitude of these costs would be enormous.

Recommendations

11. The federal and provincial governments should consider the use of a carbon tax. Given the variations of carbon content in fuels, this tax would encourage the use of cleaner fuels. It would also encourage people to make greater use of public transportation. Compensation measures should be used, though, to eliminate the potential inequities that this kind of tax could bring.

12. All levels of government should use their procurement policies to show support for the use of cleaner fuels. More specifically, the province should adopt a goal of achieving a 10% share of natural gas in new light duty vehicles by 2005. The provincial and federal governments should also require the use of 10% ethanol blends in 100% of the auto stock (except natural gas and diesel vehicles) by 1995.

---

6) Maintenance of a Car-Centred Infrastructure.

As mentioned in Section 2 of this paper, a car-centred infrastructure discourages the use of other more energy efficient modes of transportation such as public transit and bicycles. In addition, substances used to maintain this infrastructure have environmental impacts. When dissolved, road salt releases chlorine and sodium ions, which cause corrosion to roads and cars, destroy vegetation and can contaminate drinking water.[80]

7) Disposal.

Roughly 500,000 vehicles are disposed of in Ontario each year.[81] This disposal represents

---

[78] N. Myers, "Global Warming Threats", Greenpeace (1989) May/June.

[79] IPCC, Potential Impacts, 3-4.

[80] Municipal Transportation Energy and Efficiency Advisory Committee (1990), MTEEAC News, Vol. 8(4).

[81] R. Deeth, Project Manager, Shredder By-Product Berm Project, personal communication to Pollution Probe (1991).

a huge burden on Ontario's landfill sites. Even when cars are salvaged as sources of scrap metal, the non-metallic portions of the car (glass, rubber, plastic, foam, etc.) are shredded and landfilled because they "currently have no economic use".[82]

In addition, each year in Ontario 7-8 million scrap tires are generated. More than 60% of these tires end up in landfills, while an additional 10% end up in "tire piles".[83] Fewer than 700,000 annually are recycled.[84] As the recent tire fire near Hagersville, Ontario in February, 1990 has shown, tire stockpiles represent a serious threat because toxins are released into the air, terrestrial ecosystems and water tables. The Hagersville fire spewed highly toxic substances such as benzene into the air and created a runoff of thousands of litres of oil. The total cost is expected to be approximately $50 million.[85]

The disposal of car-related substances also poses serious environmental risks. The list of substances is a long one: ethylene glycol from antifreeze, hydrocarbons from transmission fluid and used oils, heavy metals from brake fluid, and sulphuric acid and lead from batteries.[86] Most of these substances are highly persistent toxins which bioaccumulate and cause massive impacts on ecosystems like the Great Lakes.[87]

---

[82] Lake Ontario Steel Company (LASCO) Ltd., Draft Environmental Assessment of Automobile Shredder By-Product Landfill (30 May 1990).

[83] Pilorusso Research Associates, Scrap Tire Management in Ontario, prepared for the Waste Management Branch, Ontario Ministry of the Environment (1991). Hereinafter: Pilorusso Research Associates, Scrap Tire Management.

[84] Ibid.

[85] "Teens Jailed for Setting Tire Blaze", Globe and Mail, 9 May 1991. Also see Ian Bailey, "Old Tire Problems Linger", London Free Press, 13 February 1991, 12; Peter Gorrie, "Legal Fights Still Smoulder", Toronto Star, 11 February 1991, 1-2,8.

[86] Elkington, The Green Consumer, op. cit.

[87] On the impact of persistent toxins on the Great Lakes, see National Wildlife Federation and the Canadian Institute for Environmental Law and Policy, A Prescription for a Healthy
(continued...)

A large percentage of lead-acid batteries are recycled to recover the lead, but this figure is declining. In the United States it has been estimated that whereas 90% of car batteries were recycled in 1979, now only 75% are recycled. This decline has been attributed to the low price received for secondary lead, which makes recycling economically unattractive.[88] The smelting of primary or secondary lead often results in the contamination of soil in industrial areas and adjoining neighbourhoods. Lead bioaccumulates in humans and can cause neurological disorders in children, even in very small doses.

Recent examples of improper disposal of other toxic substances associated with car manufacture and use include the dumping of tonnes of petroleum coke in a local quarry by Esso Petroleum Canada,[89] and a Kitchener-based oil recycler who was being charged with 26 counts of improper transportation and disposal of waste.[90] As well, a GM plant in Massena, New York was ordered by the US EPA to clean up its PCB-laden site at a cost of $130 million.[91] The roughly 55,000 truckloads of PCB-contaminated material on the site is slowly leaking into the St. Lawrence River across from Cornwall, Ontario.

---

[87](...continued)
Great Lakes: Report of the Program for Zero Discharge. (Ann Arbour and Toronto: NWF and CIELAP, 1991).

[88] Marbek Resource Consultants, Lead-Acid Batteries, briefing note to the Environmental Choice Board, Environment Canada (1990).

[89] Robert Preidt, "Trucks Dumping Oil Byproduct", Hamilton Spectator, 11 January 1991.

[90] "Oil Recycling Firm Faces 26 Charges for Waste Disposal", Kitchener-Waterloo Record, 21 November 1990.

[91] Dan Karon, "GM Told to Remove PCBs", Ottawa Citizen, 20 December 1990.

Recommendations

13. A surcharge should be applied to certain virgin materials used in cars, such as lead for lead acid batteries. This would reverse the current situation where primary lead less expensive than secondary lead. The potential for reusing rubber in tires should also be assessed, and a tax applied to the use of virgin rubber.

14. Canada should follow the example being set in Europe by designing cars for disassembly. This should include the labelling of all parts so they can be easily reused or recycled.

SECTION 4: HUMAN HEALTH COSTS

DIRECT COSTS

1) Expenditures on Road Safety.

Every year the federal government spends $15,161,000 on road safety, research and testing to prevent accidents.[92] Based on population estimates, Ontario's share of this is roughly $5 million. Despite these efforts, Canada's roads remain dangerous for car drivers. In 1988, 1,237 people were killed and 118,150 were injured in Ontario in car-related accidents.[93]

A comparative look at the safety of various modes of transportation shows that cars are by far the most dangerous way to move around. Table 3 shows an analysis of Ontario road safety statistics compiled between 1983 and 1989 by the Ontario Ministry of Transportation[94].

Table 3: Comparison of Death Rates for Buses and Cars

Mode	Deaths per 100,000 trips
Commercial buses	none
School buses	0.0007
Private car	0.02

2) Health Care Costs.

This paper explores car accident-related health care costs two ways. The first method involves the use of past statistics from bulk subrogation, or payments to OHIP by insurance

---

[92] Revenue Canada, Tax Count of Canada, 1989-90 Estimates, Part III, Expenditure Plan (1990).

[93] Ontario Ministry of Transportation and Communication, Ontario Road Safety Survey: 1988-89 (Ontario: Queen's Printer, 1989).

[94] Ibid.

companies.[95] The second method traces the path of the accident victim through the hospital, summing costs along the way. Each method has its shortcomings. However, when considered together, the two methods provide a relatively accurate picture of annual expenditures.

Using the bulk subrogation approach, the calculation of annual health care expenditures is based on the 1987 total subrogation payment of $46,843,038.[96] This total should be higher, though, given that hospital bills are likely underestimated by 25.4%,[97] that at least 13.4% of medical bills are not covered by the agreement because of contributory negligence,[98] and that 10% of accidents are not covered by the agreement.[99] Using these assumptions, it can be concluded that total car accident-related health care costs in Ontario for 1987 were $80,351,000 (in 1990 dollars).

This estimate can be checked using the second method of analysis. The advantage of following an average accident victim from the scene of the accident through to rehabilitation is that

---

[95] In 1978, OHIP and the insurance companies came to a Bulk Subrogation Agreement whereby a certain percentage of insurance premiums automatically went to OHIP. With the introduction of no-fault insurance, this agreement was cancelled. The ultimate impact was that OHIP now assumes the full cost of health care due to auto accident victims.

[96] B. Scotland (Subrogation Group, Ontario Ministry of Health), personal communication to Alex Palimaka, February 1991.

[97] The bulk subrogation estimate is too low because the costs used in 1978 to establish the agreement were much less than the costs ten years later. For more detail on this point, see the annual reports published by the Ontario Ministry of Health called Hospital Statistics. This estimate is calculated comparing 1978 and 1989 data, and takes the CPI into account.

[98] Coulter Osborne, Commissioner, Report of Inquiry into Motor Vehicle Accident Compensation in Ontario, report to the Ontario Ministry of the Attorney General and the Ontario Ministry of Financial Institutions (1988), 432. Hereinafter: Osborne, Report. It is estimated that 13.4% of the total tort losses are not compensated because they are considered by the legal system to be contributory negligence. However, these damages are still experienced by individuals who are in car accidents.

[99] B. Scotland (Subrogation Group, Ontario Ministry of Health), personal communication to Alex Palimaka, February 1991.

individual component costs can be seen. By summing annual costs in Ontario for ambulance services ($14,591,450), emergency room treatment ($2,879,245), hospital stays ($54,395,596), doctor fees ($10,824,724), and physiotherapy ($323,559), the total costs are $81,808,000.[100]

The similarity between the two estimates suggests that the cost of car-related health care during 1987 was at least $80 million (1990 dollars).

HIDDEN COSTS
1) NOx, VOCs and Ground Level Ozone.

As mentioned in Section 3, VOCs catalyze reactions between NOx and oxygen to produce ground level ozone. Elevated levels of ozone have immediate health effects including shortness of breath and coughing. Prolonged exposures for up to 6 hours at concentrations in the range of 0.08 to 0.12 ppm result in significant decreases in lung capacity and restrict the ability of affected people to absorb oxygen into the body.[101] Epidemiological studies have demonstrated a relationship between ambient air ozone concentrations and hospital admissions for acute respiratory diseases.[102]

There is also increasing concern over the long term effects of exposure to ozone. Many health professionals are concerned that exposure to ozone over a long period of time may result in permanent lung damage. Animal studies have shown that prolonged exposure to ozone can cause biochemical and structural injury to the lung.[103]

The federal government has established the acceptable ground level ozone threshold at 82

---

[100] For information on determination of dollar values, see A. Bastardi, et al, The True Cost of the Automobile, a report prepared for Pollution Probe, 144.

[101] CCME, Management Plan, op. cit., 6-7.

[102] D. Bates & R. Sizto, "Air Pollution and Hospital Admissions in Southern Ontario", Environmental Research (1987) Vol. 43: 317-331.

[103] CCME, Management Plan, op. cit.

ppb. Above this exposure level, ozone can cause damage to respiratory systems. The young, the elderly and those who already have respiratory problems are at the greatest risk.[104] For example, several studies have suggested that exposure to ozone may be associated with increased asthma attacks and hospital admissions for asthmatics.[105]

Air quality experts at Environment Canada and provincial environment ministries have collected data showing that violations of the federal ozone guideline of 82 ppb take place on a regular basis in most large Canadian cities during the summer months (see Figure 5).[106]

VOC emissions themselves also have a direct impact on human health. Many VOCs are known or suspected of having toxic effects on humans, ranging from neurotoxicity to carcinogenesis. For example, there is evidence that chronic exposure to benzene can cause leukaemia and fetal damage. VOCs are considered the probable cause of high cancer incidence in high-density traffic areas.[107]

2) Carbon Monoxide.

Carbon monoxide (CO) has a very high affinity for haemeglobin. The carboxyhaemeglobin (COHb) formed by the bonding of haemeglobin and CO is not easily broken down. The result is a decrease in the oxygen carrying capacity of blood. COHb is formed at a rate dependent upon the ambient air concentration of CO and the rate of respiration.

---

[104] Cathy Read, "Even Low Levels of Ozone in Smog Harm Lungs", New Scientist, 9 September 1989, 40.

[105] CCME, Management Plan, op. cit., 7.

[106] CCME, Management Plan, op. cit. WHO studies have shown that, internationally, Toronto rates among the highest for emissions of nitrogen dioxide. See Healthy City Office, Reconsidering the Automobile, op. cit.

[107] Committee on Biological Effects of Atmospheric Pollutants, US National Academy of Science, Airborne Lead in Perspective, (Washington, DC: National Academy of Sciences, 1972).

FIGURE 5

Number of Days per Year When Ozone Exceeded 82 ppb - average of 3 highest
years 1983-1989

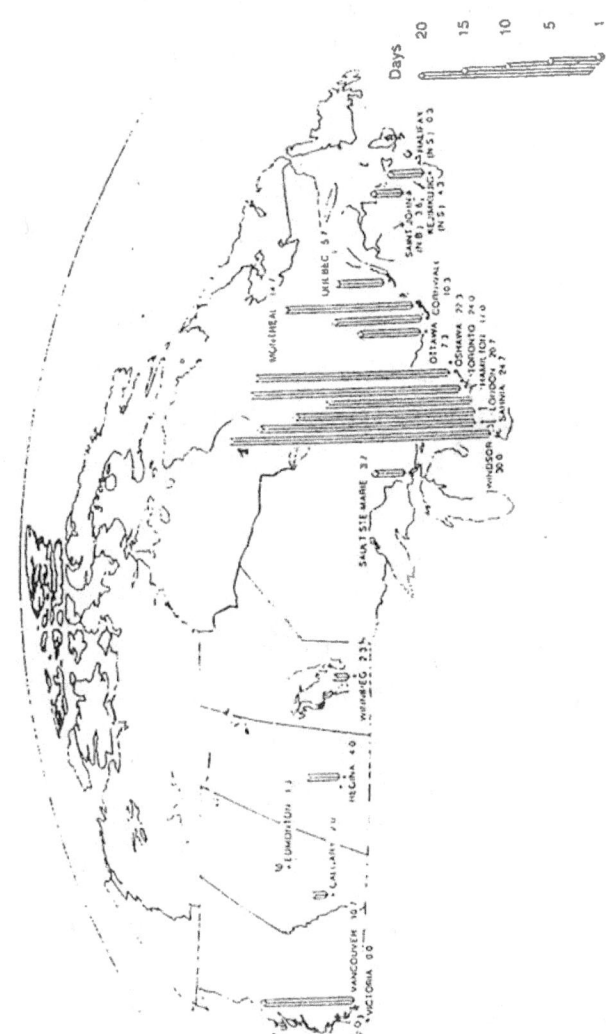

Source: CCME, Management Plan

36

A comparative look at various modes of transportation reveals the car's relative contribution to carbon monoxide emissions. See Table 4.[108]

Table 4: CO Emissions for Different Modes of Transport
(grams per 100 passenger miles)

Mode	CO Emissions
Light rail	3
Transit buses	305
Car with 3 people	502
Car with one occupant	1506

It should also be noted that some cars emit much more carbon monoxide than others. A study in the City of Toronto concluded that roughly 10% of the vehicles on the road account for more than 50% of all CO emissions.[109]

The average concentrations of carbon monoxide reported in ambient air in Toronto (2.4 ppm) do not represent a high risk to human health, according to many experts. However, the quality of air varies greatly with location and time. The Ministry of the Environment pollution readings are taken from the tops of buildings and do not necessarily reflect CO concentrations at street level. Increased levels of COHb can lead to headaches and impaired coordination in otherwise healthy people,[110] and an increase in the number of arrhythmias, commonly caused by a low oxygen supply in the blood, in heart patients.[111] Another study found that those exposed to carbon

---

[108] Marcia Lowe, "Out of the Car, Into the Future", op. cit.

[109] Healthy City Office, Evaluating the Role of the Automobile, op. cit., 88.

[110] R. Stewart, et al, Archives of Environmental Health (1970) Vol. 21: 154-164.

[111] D. Sheps, et al, "Production of Arrhythmias by Elevated COHb in Patients with Coronary Artery Disease", Annals of Internal Medicine (1990) Vol. 113(5): 343-351.

monoxide before or during exercise were three times more likely to suffer abnormal heartbeats or other cardiac irregularities.[112]

Recommendation
15. The federal and provincial governments should work with industry to take the most polluting cars off Ontario's roads. This removal program should also include the recycling of these older, inefficient cars.

---

3) Lead.

Due to its chemical immobility, lead remains in soils for a long time. Thus, even though the federal government has implemented a ban on leaded gasoline, it is important to recognize the harmful contributions these sources have made to the accumulation of lead in Canada's urban and rural environments. From 1945 to 1970 most cars were powered by leaded gasoline. Studies have shown that there is a very clear relationship between the amount of lead used in gasoline and the average blood lead levels.[113]

As well, the production of lead acid batteries for cars accounts for a substantial portion of lead emissions each year in Ontario. About 70 to 75% of lead consumption in Canada is for lead acid batteries. Lead acid batteries are made from primary or secondary lead (recovered from recycled batteries), and both primary and secondary lead smelters release lead-contaminated dust into the air and dump lead tailings into the soil. Also, lead-contaminated water drains from lead mines.[114]

Smaller, but still potent sources of car-related lead contamination are discarded automobile

---

[112] "Exercising in Polluted Air May Lead to Heart Attack", Toronto Star, 15 September 1990, G2.

[113] B. Wallace and K. Cooper, The Citizen's Guide to Lead, (Toronto: New Canada Publications, 1986) 95. Hereinafter: Wallace & Cooper, The Citizen's Guide.

[114] Commission on Lead in the Environment, Lead in the Canadian Environment: Science and Regulation. Final Report, September 1986.

batteries and lead chromate paint which is used for road markings.[115]

The body takes in most lead through the food chain and water supplies. Effects of lead in humans can be seen at even the lowest blood lead levels. Most scientists argue that there is no safe threshold level for lead; it poses a health risk at any level of exposure.[116] Children are at the greatest risk because their developing bodies are vulnerable to the mutagenic effects of lead. When measurements are made of the electrical activity in the brain, changes can be seen at blood lead levels as low as 15 micrograms/decilitre.[117] Slightly higher levels of lead are associated with decreases in IQ, problems in focusing attention and behaviour problems.[118] Lead poisoning can also affect adults; it can contribute to colic, anemia, sterility, blindness and neurological deficiencies.[119]

4) Water Pollution.

As mentioned in Section 3 of this report, petroleum refinery and chemical plant discharges have a harmful impact on Ontario's water resources. The discharge of toxins into lakes and rivers also adversely affects human health. A look at the hazards faced by the residents of Sarnia, Ontario illustrates the problem. Since 1985, Ontario's Ministry of the Environment has reported more than 350 chemical spills into Sarnia's St. Clair River, many of which contaminated the water to such an extent that downstream communities were forced to shut down their water plants temporarily.[120] If the public notification system is inadequate and residents continue to use the contaminated water, the consequences could include increased occurrences of cancer or even deaths

---

[115] Ibid.

[116] R. Goyer, "Lead Toxicity from Overt to Subclinical Subtle Health Effects", Environmental Health Perspectives (1990) Vol. 86: 177-181.

[117] Wallace and Cooper, The Citizen's Guide, op. cit., 5.

[118] Ibid.

[119] Ibid.

[120] "The Sooner the Better", London Free Press, 4 December 1990.

from poisoning. In Wallaceburg recently, some town residents remained unaware of spills of ethyl benzene, a carcinogen, from Dow Chemical's Sarnia plant.[121] Although widespread poisoning has been avoided thus far, the potential for tragedy on a large scale remains.

Given the danger of permanent contamination posed by frequent spills, a corrective pipeline is being built to supply water from Lake Huron to residents of Moore and Sombra townships in Lambton County as well as Wallaceburg, Dresden and parts of the Kent County townships of Chatham and Camden.[122] This pipeline will likely cost about $60 million to build. Since a large portion of the chemicals released into the St. Clair River in Sarnia are from petroleum refineries making fuel for cars or chemical plants making car-related products, it could be argued that about one-third of this cost, or $20 million, is related to car use in Ontario. This figure indicates the magnitude of the hidden health costs, but underestimates them, as it indicates only the cost of supplying clean water for the future, and does not reflect damage already done.

5) Ozone Depletion.

The ozone layer shields the earth against harmful ultraviolet radiation and global climate change. In addition to contributing to global warming, CFCs are responsible for destruction of the upper ozone layer.

Recent findings from the USA's National Aeronautics and Space Administration show that the ozone layer over southern Canada has decreased by 5% over a 10-year period. This means that Canadians will increasingly be exposed to harmful ultraviolet radiation.[123] This radiation

---

[121] Doug Edgar, "Warnings Issued on Spills Not Reaching Residents", Chatham Daily News, 13 November 1990.

[122] Ibid. For a chronology of the water pipeline development see the London Free Press, 1 December 1990.

[123] Earth Words: Newsletter of Friends of the Earth Canada (1991) Vol. 3(2): 1.

affects the immune system and has been linked to increased incidence of skin cancer and cataracts.[124] Each 1% loss of ozone leads to a 3-4% increase in non-melanoma skin cancer, and a 0.6% increase in cataracts.[125] In Canada, it has been predicted that one in seven Canadians will eventually contract skin cancer.[126]

6) Global Warming.

While global warming will have very serious impacts on human health and well-being over the long term, it is difficult at present to predict its specific effects on health. Still, it is essential to consider some of its most likely effects.

Changes in temperature will have a massive impact on respiratory illnesses. The effects of increased temperatures will be felt mostly by those already susceptible, like the very young and elderly, the chronically ill and those with respiratory diseases. A study using data from New York City revealed a possible average daily temperature threshold of 33 degrees Celsius, above which mortality rates, particularly for the elderly, will increase.[127]

Changes in temperature will also likely bring changes in the international distribution of diseases. Diseases such as malaria, dengue fever, yellow fever, a strain of encephalitis and Rift Valley fever which have previously been found only in tropical countries could become potential risks in North America.[128]

---

[124] Andrew Haines, "The Implications for Health", Global Warming: The Greenpeace Report, (1990) 156-57, Hereinafter: Haines, "The Implications for Health".

[125] The Standing Committee on the Environment, House of Commons, Canada, Deadly Releases: CFCs (1990).

[126] Ibid.

[127] Haines, "The Implications for Health", op. cit., 150-152.

[128] Ibid, 156.

Climate changes would have a great impact on food production. Growth in the production of food is already impaired by the effects of acid rain, ground level ozone and diminished responses to chemical fertilizers. The cumulative effect of these changes will be devastating; mortality due to malnutrition will increase, as will general illness due to weak immune systems.

Quantifying Hidden Health Costs.

Hidden health costs are extremely difficult to quantify. One study in the United States found that the cost of air pollution to the health care system was $40-$50 billion in 1985. This included costs related to asthma, lung disease, heart trouble and skin cancer. It has been estimated that a corresponding figure for Ontario would be just over $2.15 billion (1990 dollars).[129] Given that the car is responsible for approximately 30% of all air pollution[130], the car costs approximately $645 million each year in health care due to air pollution.

The amount of money spent returning water or air quality to a healthy standard can sometimes be used as an indicator of how much societies value good health. For example, the cost of the corrective pipeline to supply clean water to Wallaceburg and surrounding areas can be used to infer that society values the health of the residents as at least $60 million.

Willingness-to-pay surveys are useful for estimating how much individuals value clean air or water. This can be an indicator of the magnitude of hidden costs. For a Los Angeles study, researchers surveyed property values of houses which were equated for all measures except exposure to pollution.[131] The study found that people were paying $40 per month more to live in less polluted regions. However, Los Angeles residents have an extremely high awareness of health risks due to air pollution.

---

[129] For details, see Bastardi, et. al., The True Cost of the Automobile, op. cit.

[130] Environment Canada, Global Warming, (1990).

[131] D. Brookshire, et al, Experiments in Valuing Nonmarket Goods: A Case Study of Alternative Measures of Air Pollution Control Benefits (Washington: EPA, 1979).

A comparable study was conducted in San Francisco, where pollution from cars is much less severe than in Los Angeles and public awareness of pollution is much lower.[132] This study found that people were willing to pay about one-fifth as much as Los Angeles residents. These studies can provide a rough estimate of willingness-to-pay levels in the Greater Toronto Area. Given that Toronto's air pollution levels and public awareness lie somewhere between those of Los Angeles and San Francisco and the car is responsible for about 30% of air pollution, the willingness-to-pay for cleaner air as a result of less car emissions in the GTA would be at least $194 million annually.[133]

---

[132] E. Loehman, et al, Study Design and Property Value (Mento Park: SRI International, 1980).

[133] This figure is reached by multiplying the number of households in the GTA by $8 per month (conservatively using the willingness-to-pay of San Francisco residents), while considering currency conversions and the CPI. For more details see A. Bastardi et al, The True Cost of the Automobile, op. cit., 138.

SECTION 5: SOCIAL COSTS

DIRECT COSTS

1) Policing.

A significant percentage of police budgets are allocated to the policing of Ontario's roads. Of the $1,180 million spent by Ontario municipalities on policing in 1990, it is estimated that about $500 million goes to vehicle-related work such as enforcing road regulations.[134] Similarly, it has been estimated that almost 2/3 of the 1989 Ontario Provincial Police Marine and Traffic Unit's budget of $340 million, or $226 million, was allocated to car-related services.[135]

2) Court Costs.

Running Ontario's courts is very expensive for the provincial government. Regulation of parking and driving infractions takes up a large amount of time for the courts and its administrative apparatus. In 1987, the total number of convictions registered under the Highway Traffic Act was over 1.3 million. More than 800,000 of these convictions were related to speeding.

HIDDEN COSTS

1) Congestion and Lost Time.

A very tangible cost related to excessive car and truck use in Canadian cities is congestion and lost time. Estimates of the costs associated with congestion vary wildly.[136] One study prepared for the Ontario Ministry of Transportation on traffic in the GTA suggested that the

---

[134] Ministry of the Solicitor General Policing Services Division, Budget and Resource Analysis Summary for 1989-1990: Summary for All Forces in Ontario (1990).

[135] William Lyon (Staff Sergeant, Traffic Program, Ontario Provincial Police), personal communication to Alex Palimaka.

[136] See for example OECD, Urban Transport and the Environment (1979) in which one study estimated that the average cost for one hour of lost time in traffic congestion was worth 50% of a person's hourly wage.

economic cost of congestion and the opportunity cost to individuals and businesses could exceed $2 billion annually.

2) Stress and Decline in Quality of Life.

A fact well known by many southern Ontarians is that cars increase social stress and adversely affect quality of life. Increased numbers of cars on already crowded highways makes driving more dangerous and stressful. In addition, people who commute by car often spend long hours behind the steering wheel. This can detract from family life.

The car has other important impacts on quality of life at the neighbourhood level. For example, crossing of wide and busy streets or highways can be difficult and unsafe, and this may present barriers to certain community services or facilities. The current emphasis on a car-centred approach to urban planning means that there is little consideration of the need to foster environments, pathways and networks for cyclists and pedestrians.

3) The Transportation Disadvantaged.

Werkle and Rutherford have described in considerable detail the impact of Ontario's car-centred transportation system on those who do not have access to a car and whose needs are not met by public transit.[137] These "transportation disadvantaged" people include the elderly and disabled, women working in the suburbs and single parents. The lack of accessibility experienced when they attempt to rely on public transit may result in a reduction in individual earning potential or an inability to retain a well-paying job. As well, single parents may find it much more difficult to commute when they have to make pre- and post-work trips to day care centres via slow or crowded public transit systems.

4) Death and Injury.

Car-related accident victims become a cost to society due to loss of productivity. Although

---

[137] G. Werkle and B. Rutherford, "Employed Women in the Suburbs: Transportation Disadvantage in a Car-Centred Environment", Alternatives, (1987) Vol. 14(3).

there are problems with estimating these costs, several attempts have been made. Matheson estimated that the average annual loss of productivity was $1,357 per hospitalized victim (1985 dollars).[138] This works out to a cost of over $112 million per year (1990 dollars).[139]

Lost productivity due to car accident-related deaths has also been estimated. Matheson estimates the total costs to the Ontario economy to be approximately $620 million each year (1990 dollars).[140] Moreover, in many cases the loss of employment due to death leaves a family without a source of income, which puts demands on both provincial and federal social service systems. Lastly, there are costs associated with the emotional after-effects suffered by victims' families.

---

[138] S.O. Matheson, "Comment on the Economic Cost of Accidents" (1988) Osborne, Report, op. cit., Vol. 2: 749-757.

[139] Ibid.

[140] Ibid.

SECTION 6: ECONOMIC DEPENDENCE ON THE CAR: A BARRIER TO CHANGE

Trade-offs must be made between funding for new roads and funding for alternative modes of transport. Ontario's dependence on the auto industry and on cars themselves for transportation means that individual and government spending choices are limited.

Patterns of funding over the last 10 years graphically show which mode of transportation is favoured. The cost of building and repairing roads in Ontario has risen steadily over the past twenty years. Expensive projects in the recent past, like the construction of the 410, have been designed to accommodate increased use of the car over time. They also encourage greater reliance on the use of the car for commuting. There are no signs of a lull in highway construction; funding from the provincial government for highway 407 has been estimated to be $1.5 billion from 1987 to 2001.[141]

In contrast, Figure 6 shows that investment in rapid transit in Toronto during the 1980s slowed considerably.[142] In November 1990, the provincial government made a $5 billion commitment to rapid transit expansion in the GTA over the next 10 years by adopting most of the so-called "Let's Move" plan, and proposing some additional expenditures. A recent report by the Healthy City Office, however, puts this spending in perspective.

It states that given the lack of transit infrastructure investment in the 1980s, the "Let's Move" announcement only provides "catch up" funding.[143] If public transportation is to become the heart of Ontario's transportation policy, more funding, more research and development and

---

[141] Dan Sollovan (Engineer for the Ministry of Transportation, Planning and Design Section, Central Region), personal communication to A. Bastardi, 1991.

[142] "Rapid transit" refers to travel unobstructed by traffic, usually on rail, such as subways or the Toronto RT.

[143] Healthy City Office, Evaluating the Role of the Automobile, op. cit.

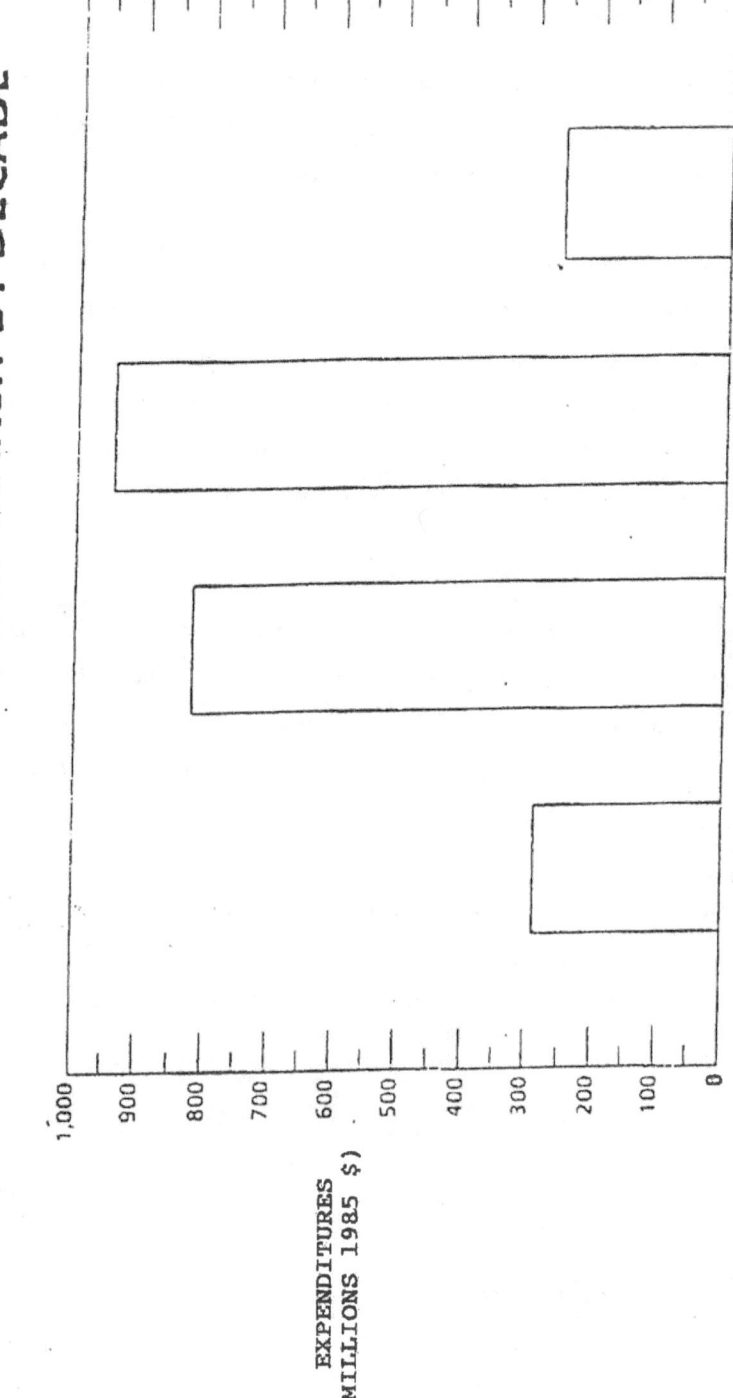

FIGURE 6

EXPENDITURES ON TTC RAPID TRANSIT BY DECADE

Source: TTC, in Healthy City Office, Evaluating the Role of the Automobile

48

most importantly more commitment is needed. This commitment will not be forthcoming if labour and governments continue to grow more dependent on the auto industry.

1) The Auto Industry

The strength of the auto industry, particularly the strength of the Big Three (GM, Ford and Chrysler), is evident in production and export figures. In 1989, the Big Three produced 886,278 of the total Canadian production of 1,001,588 passenger cars. Sales figures for the 1990 year show that 66.5% of the overall automobile sales in Canada are by the Big Three.[144] Forecasts for the 1991 year predict sales of 875,000 passenger cars.[145] Despite hard economic times, there is still a steady demand for new cars.

It has been estimated that the production and use of the automobile and the supporting activities represent over 9% of Canada's GDP.[146]

Opportunity costs are defined as opportunities and benefits foregone when expenditures are committed to specific projects or policies. For example, high opportunity costs exist when funding is focused on cars and car-related infrastructure over public transit and inter-city rail. The benefits of increasing the latter are obvious: energy savings, lower exhaust emissions and a healthier environment. However, these benefits are not being realized, and it becomes more difficult to realize them as spending becomes more committed to cars, particularly to energy inefficient cars. The auto industry encourages these opportunity costs by directly lobbying the government and by refusing to implement certain plant and car design changes which would help the environment. This lobby is very powerful with a few companies, namely the Big Three, controlling most of the auto industry.

---

[144] Geoffrey Scotton, "Foreign Autos Increase Inroads", Financial Post, 4 October 1990.

[145] K. Romain, "Car Dealers Turning Optimistic", The Globe and Mail, 14 March 1991.

[146] Statistics Canada, Catalogue 15-201, The Input-Output Structure of the Canadian Economy, 1987 (1991).

Historically, the industry has not favoured legislation imposing mandatory fuel efficiency.[147] It is crucial to note that a significant percentage of cars produced in North America have poor fuel efficiency ratings. While the average fuel efficiency for foreign cars such as Hondas, Toyotas and Volkswagons is under 7.4 litres per 100 km, the average fuel efficiency for Chryslers, GMs and Fords is 8.2-8.6 litres per 100 km.[148] In keeping with Henry Ford II's 1971 dictum that "mini-cars mean mini-profits", the Big Three have been very reluctant to phase out their larger, less efficient models.[149]

As well, the auto industry pressured Canadian governments not to require catalytic converters, and it was also reluctant to phase out the use of leaded gasoline. More recently, the auto industry lobbied against the initial proposal for a "gas guzzler" tax. In the recent Ontario budget, Treasurer Floyd Laughren proposed adding taxes on fuel inefficient vehicles.[150] For example, a $200 tax would have been added on vehicles that use more than 8.5 litres of gasoline per 100 kilometres for highway driving; the level of taxation would have increased with the level of fuel inefficiency.[151]

While this tax would have helped reduce harmful car emissions, the Motor Vehicle Manufacturers' Association of Canada accused the province of "kicking the auto industry while it is down".[152] As a result of industry pressure, the tax was changed in several important ways. It was renamed the Tax for Fuel Conservation; most cars (those with 6.0-8.9 litres/100 km fuel

---

[147] For a recent example, see "US Carmakers' Ads Slam Plans to Raise Fuel Economy Target", Toronto Star, 15 June 1991.

[148] Transport Canada Statistics, 1988.

[149] Michael Renner, "Rethinking Transportation," Worldwatch Institute, State of the World (New York: Norton & Company, 1989), 105.

[150] James Daw, "Car Makers out to Kill Guzzler Tax", Toronto Star, 15 May 1991, B1.

[151] Ibid.

[152] Ibid.

efficiencies) will only be subject to a $75 flat rate tax; rates for sport utility vehicles were reduced.

2) Labour.

Hundreds of thousands of Ontarians rely on the auto industry for employment. A car consists of about 1,300 parts assembled by many workers over an average of about 28 hours.[153] There are an estimated 111,000 jobs in Canada related to car assembly and vehicle parts manufacturing alone, 99,600 of them in Ontario.[154] An additional estimated 408,000 people were employed in May 1991 in highway, bridge and street construction and maintenance, motor vehicle and parts retailing, car-related iron and steel production and petroleum drilling and refining across Canada. About 146,100 of these jobs were located in Ontario.[155] In total, 47% of car-related jobs in Canada are located in Ontario.

3) Government Subsidies and Revenue.

The revenue generated by the auto industry, approximately $50 billion annually from car purchases, parts, accessories, insurance and gasoline,[156] and the number of workers it employs create very powerful incentives for all levels of government in Canada to support the industry. For example, GM spent $450 million upgrading its Ste-Therese plant in Quebec in 1989 and of this, 48% or $220 million came from both the provincial and federal governments.[157] In total,

---

[153] John Krafcik, "A New Diet for US Manufacturing", Technology Review (January 1989) Vol. 92(1).

[154] Statistics Canada, Catalogue 72-002, Employment, Earnings and Hours (May 1991). The 1991 figures are approximately 20% lower than for 1989, when the auto industry reached a production peak.

[155] Ibid. Labour categories included are: highway, bridge and street construction, highway and bridge maintenance, motor vehicle retail, motor vehicle parts retail, 18% of iron and steel mill employment, 18% of smelting and refining and 30% of petroleum refining and petroleum product retailing (based on car use of 18% of all steel and 30% of total refined petroleum products).

[156] Canadian Auto Association, Car Costs (1990).

[157] K. Romain, "New GM Cars May Get Axe", Globe and Mail, 21 March 1991.

51

governments have subsidized auto manufacturers with an estimated $550 million over the last decade.[158] Ontario's annual share of this amount is about $20.3 million.

The government also subsidizes drivers, albeit indirectly, by providing income tax deductions to employers who provide free or subsidized parking at the workplace. In a 1989 survey, the TTC found that 54% of non-transit-riders and light riders surveyed said they drove to work because their employer provided parking for free or at a reduced rate.[159] Similar deductions are not available to employers who provide transit passes to employees. The provincial Commercial Concentration Tax also has exemptions for companies that provide free parking.

The direct subsidization of the industry by the government is reciprocated in the form of corporate taxes. Ontario's share of corporate taxes from auto manufacturers, the petroleum industry, car dealers and people who service autos is roughly $550 million annually.[160]

The Ontario government also generates revenue from the public in the form of gas taxes and registration fees. The total revenue raised from provincial gas taxes is approximately $1.4 billion, and Ontario's share of federal gas taxes is about $880 million.[161] Registration fees for drivers and automobiles in Ontario totalled $614 million in 1989-90.[162] In addition, Ontario has a $5 tax on the purchase of each motor vehicle tire. The revenue generated by this tax is about $40 million annually.[163]

---

[158] President of AMVMA, personal communication to Pollution Probe, 20 March 1991.

[159] Healthy City Office, Evaluating the Role of the Automobile, op. cit., 105.

[160] Statistic Canada, Catalogue 61-208, Corporation Income Tax and Taxable Income: 1987 (1989).

[161] 1989-90 Ontario Budget; 1989-90 Federal Public Accounts.

[162] Ontario Chapter, Transport 2000, "Submission to the Standing Committee of the Ontario Legislature on Finance and Economic Affairs" (January 1991).

[163] Pilorusso Research Associates, Scrap Tire Management, op. cit., 114.

All of the money collected by the provincial government goes into the Consolidated Revenue Fund (CRF) and is allocated by the Treasurer of Ontario at the discretion of Cabinet. The amount of car-related revenue in the CRF has little bearing on the determination of highway expenditures, with the result that more money is often spent than raised, and that large hidden costs are not accounted for by the federal and provincial governments. Table 5 summarizes the Ontario government's car-related revenue, while Table 6 summarizes direct car-related expenditures in Ontario by various governments. These tables show the extent to which car-related spending exceeds car-related revenue in Ontario. It is important to keep in mind that the true cost of the car, including hidden costs, is significantly higher than indicated in Table 6.

Ontario Government Car-related Revenue	$ Annually (millions)
Corporate taxes	550
Provincial gas taxes	1,400
Ontario's share of federal gas taxes	880
Registration fees	614
Tire tax	40
TOTAL	3,484

Table 5: Ontario Government Annual Car-related Revenue ($ millions)

Government Car-related Expenditures in Ontario	$ Annually (millions)
Spending on highway and road construction and maintenance in Ontario by federal, provincial and municipal governments	1,900
Interest on car-related Ontario debt	1,173
Road safety and testing	5
Health care -- car accident victims	80
-- disease due to car-related air pollution	645
Policing -- Municipalities	500
-- Ontario Provincial Police	226
Subsidies to auto and oil industries	20.3+
Court Costs	n.a.
Car-related MOE spending	n.a.
TOTAL	4,549.3+

n.a. no estimates available

Table 6: Car-related Government Expenditures in Ontario

Recommendations

16. The provincial government should press the federal government to amend the Federal Income Tax Act so that companies cannot deduct the cost of providing free or subsidized parking to their employees. The provincial government should amend the Commercial Concentration Tax so that exemptions are not provided to companies that offer free parking.

    These measures should be complemented by incentives in the form of tax deductions to provide transit passes for employees, or to provide subsidized parking for HOVs.

17. Annual registration fees should be increased for second and third vehicles, especially in southern Ontario. This would provide revenue to the government to help pay for an inspection program, and would discourage multiple car ownership.

SECTION 7: THE CUMULATIVE COSTS AND IMPACTS OF THE CAR

The costs of the car to society are interrelated and cumulative. For example, emissions from cars contribute to acid rain, ozone and global warming, all of which adversely affect agriculture. As well, agriculture is adversely affected by urban sprawl, which is encouraged by the relative affordability of car travel. When all the variables are considered together, it becomes clear that the car's impact on agriculture is great.

Moreover, no region of Ontario is untouched by the costs of the car. The northern part of the province is most affected by mining for metals to make the car and materials to make roads. Production of the car's parts often takes place in small and medium size towns, like Sarnia. Likewise, the car and its parts are often disposed of in rural areas. Urban areas are most affected by tail pipe emissions and traffic congestion.

1) Costs Paid by Drivers.

Examples of the many costs paid by drivers include depreciation, insurance, registration, finance charges, unscheduled repairs and regular maintenance, gasoline, oil, tires and parking fees. In 1990, a survey done for the Canadian Automobile Association found that the average cost of owning and operating a car in Canada was $6,672.[164] The corresponding figure for Metro Toronto was $7,056.[165]

2) Direct Costs.

This paper has shown that the direct costs of the car are great. These costs include government spending on obvious items like road management. The less obvious direct costs

---

[164] Casey Mahood, "Average Cost of Keeping Car Climbs Nearly $63 a Month", Toronto Star, 2 August 1990, A7.

[165] Ibid.

55

include subsidies to car-related industries, pollution control and cleanup and health care. Examples of direct car-related costs include approximately one-third of the $60 million to build a new water pipeline because of toxins in the St. Clair river and $50 million to clean up the Hagersville tire fire, as well as the annual government expenditures listed in Table 6 at the end of Section 6.

3) Hidden Costs.

The car also imposes great hidden costs on society. Some examples of hidden costs, or figures which can be used as indicators of hidden costs, include: part of the estimated $3 billion to return 3,000 abandoned mines to "acceptable form"; $13 million in damage each year to agriculture, tourism and forestry from acidification; the estimated $14 million in crop damage each year in Ontario from elevated levels of ground-level ozone; the estimated $2 billion in lost time due to traffic congestion; and the estimated $112 and $620 million annually in lost productivity due to car-related injuries and car-related deaths, respectively.

Table 7 shows the total estimated costs attributable to the car and its supporting industries. While many costs do not have values attached to them, it is obvious that the hidden costs of the car are very large. Evidence supports the statement that the hidden costs of the car are at least as great as the direct costs of the car, and probably many times greater. With the estimates available, it can be stated that the hidden costs of the car total at least $3.7 billion, with the total costs of the car reaching over $8 billion.

A substantial amount of the costs could be saved if a concerted effort was made to reduce the use of cars in areas where public transit and bicycles are alternatives. The Canadian Urban Transit Association has found that even a modest shift from cars to transit can result in significant reductions in emissions. Table 8 shows the savings; for example, a 5% shift from car trips to transit during peak hours could save 422,605 kg of CO_2 emissions each day.[166] Ontario cannot afford to overlook the potential for public transportation to reduce emissions of greenhouse gases.

---

[166] Canadian Urban Transit Association, The Environmental Benefits of Urban Transit, a report of the Transit/Environment Task Force (April 1990), 12.

Hidden Car-related Costs	$ Annually (millions)
Loss of farmland	1,000
Environmental damage due to acid rain (20% is car-related)	13+
Plant damage due to ground level ozone	14
Global Warming (16% is car-related)	n.a.
Lost time due to traffic congestion	2,000
Stress and decline in quality of life	n.a.
Costs to transportation disadvantaged	n.a.
Lost productivity -- due to death	620
-- due to injury	11
SUB-TOTAL	**3,759+**
Government Car-related Costs (Table 6)	**4,549.3+**
TOTAL COSTS OF THE CAR	**8,308.3+**

n.a. estimate not available

Table 7. Total Estimated Costs Associated with the Car in Ontario

Area of Savings	Daily Savings
Car trips (avg. occupancy=1.3)	154,240
Hydrocarbons (VOCs) emissions	3,617 kg
Nitrogen oxide emissions	3,107 kg
Carbon dioxide emissions	422,605 kg

Source: CUTA, The Environmental Benefits of Urban transit, (April 1990).

Table 8. Projected daily car trip and emissions savings as a result of a 5% shift from peak period car trips to public transit in the Greater Toronto Area.

Bicycles are the ideal alternative with respect to energy savings and emission reduction. The US EPA has estimated that each person who cycles instead of driving alone saves per mile at least 2.6 pounds of VOCs, 20 pounds of CO, and 1.6 pounds of NOx, and 1.1 pounds of CO_2.[167] Providing bicycle paths does make a difference. When the town of Erlangen, (West) Germany created 250 km of two-wheel paths, bicycle commuting doubled.[168]

In addition, the bicycle-transit link is cost effective. The cost of providing spaces for cars and bikes at transit/subway stations differs greatly. Studies have shown that each car space requires over 300 square feet of land and costs from $4,000 to as much as $20,000 to construct, and $175 each year to maintain.[169] In contrast, each bicycle parking space uses less than 12 square feet of land at a cost of $50-$100 to build, and costs just a few dollars to maintain.[170]

---

[167] D. Gordon, Steering a New Course: Transportation, Energy and the Environment (Cambridge: Union of Concerned Scientists, 1991).

[168] Elkington, The Green Consumer, op. cit.

[169] US Department of Transportation, Urban Traffic Congestion (1987).

[170] Michael Replogle, Bicycles and Public Transportation: New Links to Suburban Transit Markets (Washington: The Bicycle Federation, 1988).

> **Recommendation**
>
> **20.** Bicycles are not just pleasure vehicles. Municipal governments should recognize the value of bicycles for commuting by creating safe bicycle paths. The TTC should provide more bicycle spaces at its stations and the public and private sector should encourage employees to bicycle to work by providing locking places and shower facilities.

Other actions can be taken to reduce the use of cars in city centres. Closing certain streets to automobile traffic completely, implementing traffic calming measures, reducing parking spaces or increasing parking fees will encourage people to find alternative modes of transportation. Studies in the US have found that either introducing paid parking where it was previously free or removing parking subsidies can reduce single-passenger driving by as much as 30%.[171]

> **Recommendations**
>
> **21.** Municipal governments should restrict the use of cars on some roads. This would make those areas more desirable for walking and shopping. People coming from outside the city centre would be encouraged to take public transit.
>
> **22.** Instead of accommodating the growing use of the car by building new roads, the province and municipalities should focus on traffic management. Traffic calming involves the use of landscaping and low speed limits to discourage the use the car.

Traffic management can also be used to make driving on main roads more fuel efficient. The use of traffic signals designed to respond to the flow of traffic can reduce unnecessary idling, stopping and starting. The Ontario Ministry of Transportation estimates that up to 20% of all emissions could be reduced through better coordination of traffic signals and improved signal timing.[172]

---

[171] Thomas Higgins, "Guidelines for Developing Local Demand Management or Trip Reduction Policies", presented at the 69th Annual Transportation Research Board Meeting (1990).

[172] Healthy City Office, Evaluating the Role of the Automobile, op. cit., 97.

> **Recommendation**
> **23.** Travel on main roads should be made more efficient through the use of modern signal equipment. This would reduce car emissions due to unnecessary frequent starting and stopping.

One hidden cost which is even more difficult to quantify is the opportunity cost arising from Ontario's economic dependence on the auto industry. Funding is not easily transferred to other sectors, such as research and development on better forms.of public transit, alternative fuels, or better urban-rural planning. As the auto industry grows, as more jobs are dependent upon it and the industry lobby grows more powerful, it will be increasingly difficult to come by funding and political commitment for alternative forms of transportation.

The recommendations in this report are aimed at industry, business, individuals and all levels of government. The most important changes can be made at the individual level. By working from home, riding a bicycle to work or taking public transit, every one can contribute to reducing harmful car emissions. Some of these recommendations may appear to involve major lifestyle changes. However, a Maclean's-Decima Poll taken in August 1990 revealed that 62% of Canadians would be willing to drive their car 50% less to reduce global warming.[173] With this degree of public awareness and commitment to the environment, Pollution Probe feels that political commitment will increase and the recommendations made throughout this report are realistic and achievable.

---

[173] "Hopes and Fears: people are prepared to change", Maclean's, 17 September 1990, 44.

Recommendations

24. With the proliferation of communications technology, substantial energy and emission savings can be realized by combining home and the workplace. Employers should encourage working from home whenever possible.

25. An education program should be launched by the provincial government to inform drivers of the car's impact on human health and the environment. A program similar to the drinking and driving campaign would be extremely effective in showing how much the car truly costs society.

26. Individuals should consider the hidden costs of the car when making decisions on lifestyle. Deliberately leaving the car at home one or two days a week would gradually reduce dependence on the car and would increase public transit ridership, thereby encouraging transit officials to improve their systems.

REFERENCES

Bastardi, A., et al, The True Cost of the Automobile, A Report Prepared for Pollution Probe (April 1991).

Bates, D. and R. Sizto, "Air Pollution and Hospital Admissions in Southern Ontario", Environmental Research (1987) Vol. 43, 317-331.

Brookshire, D., et al, Experiments in Valuing Nonmarket Goods: A Case Study of Alternative Measures of Air Pollution Control Benefits (Washington: EPA, 1979).

Bruce, James, "Myths and Realities of Global Climate Change", Ecodecision (1991) Vol. 1(1).

Byers, J., "Development Freeze Urged for Farmland", Toronto Star, 6 June 1991, A12.

Canadian Auto Association, Car Costs (1990).

Canadian Council of Ministers of the Environment, Management Plan for NOx and VOCs, Phase I, (November 1990).

Canadian Urban Transit Association, The Environmental Benefits of Urban Transit, a report of the Transit/Environment Task Force, April 1990.

Commission on Lead in the Environment, Lead in the Canadian Environment: Science and Regulation, Final Report, September 1986.

Committee on Biological Effects of Atmospheric Pollutants, US National Academy of Sciences, Airborne Lead in Perspective, (Washington, DC: National Academy of Science, 1972).

Daw, James, "Car Makers Out to Kill Guzzler Tax", Toronto Star, 15 May 1991, B1.

Edgar, Doug, "Warnings Issued on Spills Not Reaching Residents", Chatham Daily News, 13 November 1990.

Elkington, John, et al, The Green Consumer (New York: Penguin, 1990).

Environment Canada, Emission Trends of Common Air Contaminants in Canada: 1970-1980 (1984).

Environment Canada, Arctic Haze: Visible Air Pollution (1989).

Environment Canada, Global Warming (1990).

"Exercising in Polluted Air May Lead to Heart Attack", Toronto Star, 15 September 1990, G2.

Federal/Provincial Research and Monitoring Coordinating Committee, The 1990 Canadian Long-Range Transport of Air Pollutants and Acid Deposition Assessment Report, Parts I & V, (1990).

Flanders, John, "Big Spill Could Devastate Great Lakes: New Report", Hamilton Spectator, 3 November 1990.

Friedman, R. et al, Urban Ozone and the Clean Air Act, (Office of Technology Assessment, 1988).

George, J. and B. Blackwelder, "Oil Fires: A Mideast Chernobyl?", Toronto Star, 10 July 1991.

"Goodyear Closes in Owen Sound", Kingston Whig Standard, 24 September 1990.

Gordon, D., Steering a New Course: Transportation, Energy and the Environment (Cambridge: Union of Concerned Scientists, 1991).

Gorrie, Peter, "Lake Fuel Spill Just a Warning", Toronto Star, 20 May 1991.

Goyer, R., "Lead Toxicity from Overt Subclinical Subtle Health Effects", Environmental Health Perspectives (1990) Vol. 86, 177-181.

The Green Transportation Campaign, Greening Ontario's Transportation: A Public Campaign (1991).

Greenpeace International, The Environmental Impact of the Car (1991).

Haines, Andrew, "The Implications for Health", Global Warming: The Greenpeace Report (1990).

Healthy City Office, City of Toronto & The Technical Working Group on Traffic Calming and Vehicle Emission Reduction, Evaluating the Role of the Automobile: A Municipal Strategy (September 1991).

Herron, Shaun, "Refinery Under Investigation Over Sulphur Gas Emission", Hamilton Spectator, 10 October 1990.

63

Higgins, Thomas, "Guidelines for Developing Local Demand Management or Trip Reduction Policies", presented at the 69th Annual Transportation Research Board Meeting (1990).

"Hopes and Fears: people are prepared to change", Maclean's, 17 September 1990, 44.

Hume, C., "U.S. Expert Fears Cars Will Ruin Amazing Metro", Toronto Star, 1 May 1991, A1.

Intergovernmental Panel on Climate Change, Potential Impacts of Climate Change (1990).

Karon, Dan, "GM Told to Remove PCBs", Ottawa Citizen, 20 December 1990.

Krafcik, John, "A New Diet for US Manufacturing", Technology Review (January 1989) Vol. 92(1).

Lake Ontario Steel Company Ltd., Draft Environmental Assessment of Automobile Shredder By-Product Landfill (30 May 1990).

Leggett, Jeremy, "The Nature of the Greenhouse Threat", Global Warming: The Greenpeace Report (1990).

Loehman, E. et al, Study Design and Property Value (Mento Park: SRI International, 1980).

Lowe, Marcia, "Out of the Car, Into the Future", World Watch (November/December 1990) 21.

Macdonald, Doug, The Politics of Pollution (Toronto: McClelland & Stewart, 1991).

Mahood, Casey, "Average Cost of Keeping Car Climbs Nearly $63 a Month", Toronto Star, 2 August 1990, A7.

Marbek Resource Consultants, Lead-Acid Batteries, briefing note to the Environmental Choice Board, Environment Canada (1990).

Matheson, S. O., "Comment on the Economic Cost of Accidents", Report of Inquiry into Motor Vehicle Accident Compensation in Ontario (1988).

McCormick, John, Acid Earth: The Global Threat of Acid Pollution (London: Earthscan and IIED, 1985).

McLaughlin, D., et al, Sugar Maple Decline in Ontario (Ministry of the Environment, 1987).

Municipal Transportation Energy and Efficiency Advisory Committee (1990) <u>MTEEAC News</u>, Vol. 8(4).

Myers, N., "Global Warming Threats", <u>Greenpeace</u> (May/June 1989).

Newman, P. and J. Kenworthy, <u>Cities and Automobile Dependence</u> (Sydney: Gower Technical, 1989).

"Oil recycling Firm Faces 26 Charges for Waste Disposal", <u>Kitchener-Waterloo Record</u>, 21 November 1990.

Ontario Government, <u>1989-90 Ontario Budget</u> (1990).

Ontario Environment Network, <u>Sustainability As If We Mean It</u>, Position Paper prepared for the Ontario Roundtable on the Environment and the Economy (April 1991).

Ontario Global Warming Coalition, Philip Jessup, et al, eds., <u>Degrees of Change: Steps Towards an Ontario Global Warming Strategy</u>, prepared for the Ontario Ministries of Energy and the Environment (June 1991).

Ontario Ministry of Energy, <u>Ontario Energy Review</u> (1990).

Ontario Ministry of the Environment, <u>Report on the 1988 Industrial District Discharges in Ontario</u> (1989).

Ontario Ministry of the Environment, <u>Second Report on the Monitoring Data for the Petroleum Refining Sector</u> (1990).

Ontario Ministry of the Solicitor General, Policing Services Division, <u>Budget and Resource Analysis Summary for 1989-1990: Summary for All Forces in Ontario</u> (1990).

Ontario Ministry of Transportation and Communication, <u>Ontario Road Safety Survey: 1988-89</u> (Ontario: Queen's Printer, 1989).

Ontario Roundtable on the Environment and the Economy, "Energy and Mineral Task Force Consultation Document" (May 1991).

Organisation for Economic Co-operation and Development, <u>Urban Transport and the Environment</u> (1979).

Osborne, Coulter, Commissioner, <u>Report of Inquiry into Motor Vehicle Accident Compensation in Ontario</u>, report to the Ontario Ministry of the Attorney General and the Ontario Ministry of Financial Institutions (1988).

Pilorusso Research Associates, <u>Scrap Tire Management in Ontario,</u> prepared for the Waste Management Branch of the Ontario Ministry of the Environment (1991).

Pollution Probe, et al, <u>The Canadian Green Consumer Guide</u> (Toronto: McClelland & Stewart, 1990).

Pollution Probe, "Greening Canada's Passenger Transportation System", brief presented to the Royal Commission on National Passenger Transportation (July 1990) 19-20.

Preidt, Robert, "Trucks Dumping Oil Byproduct", <u>Hamilton Spectator</u>, 11 January 1991.

Read, Cathy, "Even Low Levels of Ozone in Smog Harm Lungs", <u>New Scientist</u> (9 September 1989), 40.

Renner, Michael, <u>Rethinking the Role of the Automobile</u>, Worldwatch Institute Paper #84 (1988).

Renner, Michael, "Rethinking Transportation", Worldwatch Institute, <u>State of the World</u> (New York: Norton & Company, 1989), 105.

Rennie, Gary, "Grier Blasts Dow Over Spills", <u>Windsor Star</u>, 7 November 1990.

Replogle, Michael, <u>Bicycles and Public Transportation: New Links to Suburban Transit Markets</u> (Washington: The Bicycle Federation, 1988).

Revenue Canada, <u>Tax Count of Canada, 1989-90 Estimates, Part III, Expenditure Plan</u> (1990).

Romain, K., "Car Dealers Turning Optimistic", <u>Globe and Mail</u>, 14 March 1991.

Romain, K., "New GM Cars May Get Axe", <u>Globe and Mail</u>, 21 March 1991.

Saab, "How to Maintain Your Car and Environmental Conscience" (1991).

Sanderson, Marie, "Implications of Climatic Change for Navigation and Power Generation in the Great Lakes" (Environment Canada, 1987).

Scotton, Geoffrey, "Foreign Autos Increase Inroads", <u>Financial Post</u>, 4 October 1990.

Sheps, D., et al, "Production of Arrhythmias by Elevated COHb in Patients with Coronary Artery Diseases", <u>Annals of Internal Medicine</u> (1990) Vol. 113(5), 343-351.

Small, Peter, "TTC Plan to Restrict Traffic Draws Some Motorist Approval", <u>Toronto Star</u>, 3 April 1991.

"The Sooner the Better", London Free Press, 4 December 1990.

Spears, Tom, "Waste Cleanup Will Need $3 Billion", Ottawa Citizen, 25 October 1990.

The Standing Committee on the Environment, Deadly Releases: CFCs, (1990).

Statistics Canada, Canada Year Book (Ottawa: Statistics Canada, 1989).

Statistics Canada, Catalogue 26-225 Quarries and Sand Pits (1985).

Statistics Canada, Catalogue 57-208 Consumption of Purchased Fuel and Electricity: 1984 (1987).

Statistics Canada, Catalogue 41-001 Primary Iron and Steel (December 1989).

Statistics Canada, Catalogue 61-208 Corporation Income Tax and Taxable Income: 1987 (1989).

Statistics Canada, Catalogue 57-003 Quarterly Report on Energy Supply-Demand in Canada (1990iv).

Statistics Canada, Catalogue 15-201 The Input-Output Structure of the Canadian Economy, 1987 (1991).

Statistics Canada, Catalogue 72-002 Employment, Earnings and Hours (1991).

Stokoe, Peter, Socio-Economic Assessment of the Physical and Ecological Impacts of Climate Change on the Marine Environment of the Atlantic Region of Canada (Environment Canada, 1988).

"Teens Jailed for Setting Tire Blaze", Globe and Mail, 9 May 1991.

Transport 2000, Ontario Chapter, "Submission to the Standing Committee of the Ontario Legislature on Finance and Economic Affairs" (January 1991).

Transport Canada, A Plan to Identify and Assess Emission Reduction Opportunities from Transportation, Industrial Engines and Motor Fuels (1989)

"Uniroyal Wants to Dump More Waste on This Community, But Still Refuses to Accept Responsibility for Past Mess", Elmira Independent, 5 November 1990.

United States Department of Transportation, Urban Traffic Congestion (1987).

Wall, G., "Implications of Climatic Change for Tourism and Recreation in Ontario"

(Environment Canada, 1988).

Wallace, B. and K. Cooper, <u>The Citizen's Guide to Lead</u>, (Toronto: New Canada Publications, 1986), 95.

Werkle, G. and B. Rutherford, "Employed Women in the Suburbs: Transportation Disadvantage in a Car-Centred Environment", <u>Alternatives</u>, (1987) Vol. 14(3).

Winston, Clifford, "How to Ease Traffic Jams" <u>New York Times</u>, 18 July 1990.

Woodwell, George, "The Effects of Global Warming", <u>Global Warming: The Greenpeace Report</u>, J. Leggett, ed. (New York: Oxford U. Press, 1990).

Notes on the Contributors

David McRobert was the Global Warming Program Coordinator at Pollution Probe when this report was written. He now works at the Waste Reduction Office at the Ontario MOE. He holds a B.Sc. in Biology from Trent University, an MES from York, and LLB from Osgoode Hall Law School. Mr. McRobert has been involved in research and advocacy on environmental issues for more than ten years and he is an avid bike rider.

Greg Hein was also a researcher at Pollution Probe. He holds a B.A.H. from Queen's University and an M.A. from the University of British Columbia. Mr. Hein is a doctoral candidate in the Department of Political Science, University of Toronto.

Alex Palimaka has completed a B.Sc. at the University of Toronto.
He is currently doing contract work for the City of Toronto's Environment Committee on the cost of private car use. Mr. Palimaka is also attending York University in the joint LLB-MES program.

Tija Luste recently completed a B.A. in Environment and Resource Management and Economics at the University of Toronto, and is in the process of applying to graduate schools for the fall of 1992.

About Pollution Probe

The Pollution Probe Foundation, founded in 1969, is one of Canada's most effective public interest groups. Through research and advocacy programs on issues like water pollution, waste management, zero discharge and global warming, Pollution Probe encourages individuals, corporations, communities and governments to adopt pragmatic solutions to our most pressing environmental problems. Projects such as the publication of The Canadian Green Consumer Guide have provided Canadians with ready access to information they need on how to protect the environment.

Pollution Probe is a registered charitable organization, supported by tax deductible donations from corporations, foundations and individuals and by income earned from publication sales, government contracts for special projects and public education programs.

Find out more about Pollution Probe and offer your support. Write to:

Pollution Probe
12 Madison Ave.
Toronto, Ont.
M5R 2S1

(416) 926-1907

October 23, 1991

NDP CONFERENCE SHOULD FOCUS ON "HOW" TO REDUCE CAR DEPENDENCY,
NOT DITHER WONDERING "IF" IT CAN BE DONE

Participants in the NDP Environment Committee's Conference on
The Automobile should stop loitering in the showroom and start
making the hard choices needed to reduce our ecologically
unaffordable dependency on cars, Pollution Probe said today.

"Ontario simply has to break the economic chains which bind it
to the automobile," said Pollution Probe's Paul Muldoon.

"Taxpayers can't afford to continue funding a billion-dollar-a-
year subsidy to the car. Citizens can't continue to risk their
health. The environment can't continue to take the punishment a
car-centred society dishes out to our air, our waterways and
our land," he said.

Pollution Probe is asking the municipal and provincial
officials, academics, and those involved in the auto industry
who will be attending the NDP Environment Committee conference
this weekend to think creatively in defence of the environment,
and not in defence of the transportation status quo.

Environmental knowledge has moved well beyond the rhetorical
question asked in the conference's promotional literature: "Can
we reduce our dependency on the auto with a more diversified
approach to transportation?"

"Of course we can reduce our car-addiction, and the attendees
at this conference owe it to the people of Ontario to make that
clear, and to start suggesting to the government how to do it,"
Mr. Muldoon said.

Pollution Probe made 26 recommendations on how to get the job
rolling in its report "The Costs of the Car" which it released
today. Among the recommendations:

    o   The Ontario government should abandon the car-dependent
Seaton suburb scheme and change land use rules to require that
public transit investment go hand-in-hand with new development.

    o   Automobile manufacturers should follow the example of
European car-makers and design cars to be readily disassembled
into reusable and recyclable parts when their useful life is
over.

    o   The Ontario and Federal governments should require by
law that as of 1995, all gasoline sold should contain 10% ethyl
alcohol to reduce air pollution.

o   Municipal governments should recognize that the bicycle
is a useful, non-polluting form of transportation which needs
to be encouraged by designating special bicycle paths and
lanes.

o   The Federal government should encourage auto parts
recycling by taxing the car manufacturing uses of certain
virgin materials, such as lead in batteries.

"Most of all, the provincial government should face up to the
fact that it is massively subsidizing air pollution, resource
depletion and urban sprawl by spending a billion dollars a year
more on the automobile than it receives in car related taxes,"
Pollution Probe researcher Tija Luste said.

"It's crazy, but for decades the provincial government has been
paying drivers to pollute," she said.

The Pollution Probe report shows that the Ontario Government
takes in $3.5 billion annually in car-related revenue,
including gasoline taxes ($2.3 billion), registration and
license fees ($0.6 billion), and auto industry corporate taxes
(0.6 billion).

The province spends $4.5 billion on car-related costs,
including highway construction and maintenance ($1.9 billion),
interest on the car-related portion of the provincial debt
($1.2 billion), health care for accident victims ($80 million)
and car-caused air pollution sufferers ($645 million), and
traffic policing ($726 million).

The report also enumerates the hidden costs of Ontario's car
dependency. Among these costs:

o   Air pollution. Motor vehicles are responsible for 16%
of Ontario's human-generated global warming gases such as
carbon dioxide and methane.

o   Air pollution. Motor vehicles are responsible for 13%
of all the acid rain-causing sulfur dioxide and nitrogen oxides
emitted in the province.

o   Air pollution. Motor vehicles are responsible for 20%
of smog-producing ground-level ozone. They emit fully one-third
of all the gases causing Toronto and other Southern Ontario
cities to be socked in by smog several times each summer. (How
unneccesary is the high environmental cost of transportation?
Transit buses are 2 1/2 times less polluting than single
passenger cars, subways are six times less polluting.)

o   Safety. Each year, 1,200 people are killed and 118,000
injured in automobile accidents. Lost productivity from these
deaths and injuries totals $732 million annually.

o   Resource depletion. The automobile alone guzzles 31% of the nation's refined petroleum output.

While the way is clear -- we must re-channel much of the tax monies now spent to subsidize the automobile into public transit investment -- Ontario has a problem. The automobile industry is a big part of the provincial economy.

"As the auto industry grows, as more jobs are dependent upon it and the industry lobby grows more powerful, it will be increasingly difficult to come by funding and political commitment for alternative forms of transportation," the report notes.

"That's why this weekend's conference is so important. The environment committee of the ruling party is meeting to discuss the car. Surely we can count on an NDP government to stop subsidizing pollution.

"Pollution Probe is calling on the attendees -- people from municipalities, the New Democratic Party, and auto workers themselves -- to squarely face up to the basic environmental truth that governments which spend money on polluting forms of transportation are tossing away opportunities to invest in cleaner ones," Mr. Muldoon said.

- 30 -

For further information:

Paul Muldoon, Pollution Probe   (416) 926-1907
Tija Luste, Pollution Probe   (416) 926-1907